A Special Journey

Getting to know my father
&
the men he flew with.

Rosemary Edmeads

GHP

**Grosvenor House
Publishing Limited**

This book is published by
Grosvenor House Publishing Ltd
28-30 High Street, Guildford, Surrey, GU1 3EL.
www.grosvenorhousepublishing.co.uk

A CIP record for this book
is available from the British Library

ISBN 978-1-78148-727-3

Book cover design by Robert Reichert

DEDICATED

To the airmen of Halifax JP 162 FS
"S for sugar"… Still on Sortie August 4th/5th 1944.

Seven strangers thrown together by circumstance
Who stayed together by choice
And flew together as a crew.
An efficient and effective team relying on each other on
the missions they flew.
Seven brave airmen to those who knew them
and to those who have come to know them.
We are so very proud.

This is just one story, of one man, and the aircrew he flew with
so many years ago. As I think of the sacrifice that my father
made. I also think of the two airmen who died with him that
night and the other four brave airmen who spent many months
evading capture before returning home.

There were so many other men who did not return on that
August 4/5 Mission 1944. Families, who like mine, were left
behind, so many men who lost their lives.

This story is about one of them "he was my father."

CONTENTS

Part One

My Fathers Life February 17th 1911 to August 5th, 1944.

Part Two
Journey to Krakow

FORWARD

Rosemary Edmeads and I were both schoolgirls at the same school in the city of Lancaster for a brief time in the late 1950's and yet I have no recollection of her, or she of me. That is a pity because if we had only known it, we shared so much. Every now and then our separate lives almost converged, only to veer away on a different course at the last moment. And yet we would meet each other eventually - not in the places we had shared - Morecambe, Lancaster or Helensburgh, but in St. Clement Danes Church in the Strand, London, for a service to honour the men of the Special Duty Squadrons.

We are both daughters of RAF Voluntary Reserve airmen who served with 148 Special Duty Squadron, flying supplies and agents into the Balkans and Poland during 1944. One of our fathers survived, the other did not. It was Rosemary's father, Air Gunner John Frederick Cairney Rae who didn't make it – shot out of the sky by a Luftwaffe fighter pilot whilst attempting to fly supplies to the Polish Home Army during the first days of the Warsaw Uprising in August 1944. Rosemary would never know the joy of being held in her father's arms or hear his laughter. She would, throughout her life, imagine his love for her but never experience it.

His death came at a critical point of the war on the Eastern Front. The Russian Army had reached the outskirts of Warsaw and was in a position to assist the Polish Home Army as they rose up to retake the City. Except that they did not assist. They stood back and watched as Warsaw burned; the Uprising crushed by an overwhelming force, whilst Polish, South African and Commonwealth aircrews, flying a round trip of more than two thousand miles from bases in Italy, tried to help. It was an impossible task and yet night after night they flew to Krakow, or Warsaw itself, in an attempt to drop vital ammunition and supplies to the beleaguered men and women fighting for their lives in the streets below. The task was a hopeless one and many crews were lost in this forlorn but gallant attempt to help the freedom fighters of the Home Army. It was a dark period of the War, described by Sir John Slessor, Deputy Commander of Allied air forces in the Mediterranean as "the utmost gallantry and self-sacrifice on the part of our aircrews and the blackest-hearted, coldest-blooded treachery on the part of the Russians". Historians have written much of the betrayal and abandonment of the Polish Underground Army, but this story shines a spotlight on the honourable actions of the crews who did their best to help, and the principled actions of the Polish Partisans, who rescued and hid Allied airmen at great personal cost.

The Halifax flew with a crew of seven and they were a tight knit group, who not only flew together but spent off-duty hours in each other's company. It is therefore fitting that Rosemary has researched the lives of each crewmember, four of whom survived and three who perished on that dreadful night. Where this story differs from the purely historical, is in its personal telling of the residual effect of war – the broken lives and ongoing sense of loss. A second tragic loss, at the age of fourteen, changed her life forever and the following years – spent in the bustling seaside town of Morecambe, were troubled and sometimes lonely. Rosemary has waited a long time to tell this story and because of that, she has been able to reflect on the affect her father's death has had on her own life with great clarity and insight. It is tempting as a writer to edit or reconstruct facts in a biographical account, but you get the feeling that, in this particular story, the flood gate has opened and out has poured the truth.

I have been to the place where John Rae and two of his comrades are laid to rest, in the Rakowicki Cemetary, Krakow, and can still recall the birdsong and distant toll of church bells in that peaceful resting ground. It is a place where sacrifice is honoured.

Their story needed to be written.

Jennifer Elkin

PREFACE

Seventy years have passed since the disastrous night of August 4/5th 1944 when life for my mother Alice Rae and I changed forever.

Throughout my life as I have met and been introduced to new people the usual general questions have been asked and answered in conversations. In California where I now live, the first question I am usually asked is "Where are you from?" I believe this often with reference to my English accent but as I always reply "I am not the one with the accent!!" But I should continue on a more serious note.

The question I find hardest to answer is when I am asked about my parents. I do respond to this without making the questioner feel embarrassed or sorry that they had asked; I try to explain very simply my circumstances of loosing my parents. This was and still is sometimes hard to do because I did not, and still do not, know the complete story. As I write this I have tried to fill in all the missing pieces but that has not always been possible.

I have, without realizing, become the family historian. I needed to make this journey of discovery to try to answer the many questions I had as I was growing up that needed to be answered and certainly there seem to be even more urgency to have them answered as I grow older. My files grew and I realized that the generations of Ray/Rae's I had come to know through my research were also people who also had suffered loss and hardships but had become all the stronger for having done so.

When I finally turned my attention to the father I never knew, John Rae, who served his country in a time of need and died doing so, my admiration for him and for the family he came from grew.

Questions are still directed at me but they are different questions "What are you going to do with all the information you have gathered?" "Have you written your story down—it needs to be told." "I have decided to begin."I reply. "I am trying to write it down for my daughters and my grandsons, but I am not sure they will read it." "Why is that?" I am asked? "I think maybe they do not want to think of what happened to my mother and I after my dad, their grandfather was killed." "They will want to read it someday" is their response. "Yes, perhaps. Maybe when I am no longer here."

By telling his story and that of the airmen he flew with I hope that I can honor them in some small way and make my dad proud.

INTRODUCTION

There's a clever phrase "this story is a true story about something that happened a long time ago, cited in the present."

The crashing of Halifax JP162FS-S near the village of Niecew in Poland nearly seventy years ago was my starting point in this long journey I have taken and in the process it has helped me get to know my father. In effect it is part of the history of World War 11, which was called the "Air Battle over Europe." To the Underground fighters in Poland it was called the "the Battle for Warsaw" and only after the city was destroyed did it become known as the Warsaw Uprising, events in the Second World War of which I, and most of the Allied population knew nothing about. My journey back to the past led me to remember the missions conducted over Poland by Special Duties Squadrons one of which was Royal Air Force 148 Squadron.

This is the story of a Royal Air Force bomber Halifax JP162FS-S dropping not bombs but much needed supplies to the partisans who were fighting so heroically during the German occupation and at the beginning of the Warsaw Uprising. The story of the aircrew in that plane which along with six other airplanes from 148 Special Duties Squadron and seven from the 1586 Polish Squadron, flew from their base in Brindisi, in the South of Italy on the night of August 4/5th 1944. From there they flew over war torn Europe to a tiny "drop zone" in occupied Poland. A mission, as I have said to aid the Polish AK (Armia Krajowa) Home Army. It was to be an ill-fated mission.

As well as recounting the story of this particular mission I will also be journeying into the histories of the members of the aircrew of the Halifax JP162FS-s which was sent to this particular "drop zone." Theses drop zones were distant from Warsaw because the RAF commanders thought that this would be safer than flying to Warsaw with their supplies, but these airmen were nevertheless risking their lives on the flight to and on the return flight.

These airmen believed in the justice of their assignment and suffered a heavy toll. Of the twenty-eight airmen on four RAF aircraft which failed to return, seventeen were killed, seven became prisoners of war but amazingly four, from my father's plane, with the aid of the partisans avoided capture and eventually reached England. For these airmen joining the AK was to continue the fight against the Germans not as they had been trained to do in the air but as guerrillas on land. It was that or be turned over to the German Army. To these airmen joining the AK army seemed the better option.

It has taken me several years to piece together the story of this crew and the many missions they flew together. At times it has been a struggle but one I have not been willing to abandon. As long as I am busy finding information about them their memory is kept alive and they are not forgotten.

On July 25, 2013 I began the long journey from my home in Southern California where I now live to Krakow to trace their journey and meet with people who would hopefully help me complete my journey into my father's life and discover the full story about that fateful flight in 1944. All of these people were connected in different ways to that flight and its supply drop to the AK. I was able to make contact with these wonderful people in my extensive searches for information about my father's last mission. Their research and sometimes first hand knowledge and experience filled the story of the last flight of Halifax

JP162 and of the partisans he was trying to help in their uprising against the German forces. Their kindness and generosity to a complete stranger has at times been overwhelming and I began this journey full of hope, full of excitement to meet these "strangers." Yet despite all this kindness, hope and excitement I have many reservations about my journey.

This is the story of one airplane and one special man on that plane my father, Sergeant John Frederick Cairney Rae, RAFVR, who had the lonely job as Rear Gunner. Alone in his tiny cramped and isolated turret without even enough room for a parachute but with the heavy responsibility of providing protection for his crew.

PART ONE

MY FATHER

HIS LIFE AND SERVICE

FEBRUARY 17 1911 to AUGUST 5 1944

CHAPTER 1

EARLY BEGININGS

As I begin my story I should tell you a little of this family called Ray/Rae. Sometime about the turn of the 19th century the Rays became Rae's. It was probably a simple error on the part of the registrar or census taker, all records in the 1900's were manual and mistakes once made where perpetuated.

The Rays appear to be to have been a very proud strong even adventurous family. My research established they could be found living in the same area around Govan situated on the River Clyde in the Glasgow area on the West coast of Scotland. To this day the area is still home to many Rae families all connected in some way.

As I traced the family history searching the census records I came across something unexpected. In 1881 in the United Kingdom a National Census[1] was taken. These Census records show my grandfather Martin Ray's name and those of his siblings were still living at home at 19 Victoria Street, Govan, Lanark, Scotland. What was so exciting about this routine entry was their place of birth.....listed as the East Indies and their father, my great grandfather, Michael Ray was listed as a "Chelsea Pensioner." This was all very intriguing. I was not sure where the East Indies were and I was curious as to why this should be. As I explored further it was suggested that he may have worked for the East India Company. This proved to be a false trail. Why a Chelsea Pensioner? Surely these are the stately old soldiers in the quaint red uniforms who live in the Chelsea

Hospital in London and are much on display during the prestigious Chelsea Flower Show? I contacted the Chelsea Pensioner Association and discovered that all Army Pensions at that time were distributed by their organization. Not all pensioners were "live-in." Most men who retired from the army were 'live-out" pensioners and resided in their local communities.

From this starting point I found that Michael Ray, my great grandfather, at age 20, and his young bride Catherine age 18 were married on May 9th, 1853 at St Patrick's Church in Glasgow[2] after the banns had been read. They set sail from their home town of Glasgow for Madras, India in December 1853 on the Steam Ship Lissmoyne[3] on the long sea journey. Michael had enlisted in an Indian Regiment the 3rd Madras Fusiliers for ten years. This regiment was one of the East India Companies regiments i.e. not under the control of the British Crown, so although not a direct member of the East India Company Michael was in effect employed by them. In 1857 he fought in the Indian Mutiny. This tragic conflict revealed the failings of the East India Company and the British Parliament stripped it of its power in India and the regiment of the company, along with all the other regiments of the company, became part of the Indian Army under the direct control from Britain in 1861. Michael Ray was awarded the India Mutiny medal for his service in Central India. He then re enlisted in 1863 or as they say "took the Queen's Shilling.[4]" Queen Victoria was then on the throne and Michael served for a further ten years as a Private in the Sub- Continent in a British Regiment the Royal Artillery. Michael and Catherine lived in India for twenty years in all, raising ten children[5]. They returned in 1873 or 1874 to settle back in Govan with eight of their children. Michael was awarded a pension of one shilling a day for his long service.[6]

The family settled down to life and I am sure that the children must have found the life in this area of Scotland vastly different to the one they had left behind when they were living in India. There they were constantly on the move with their father's regiment, living in a hot and sometime inhospitable climate.

Their youngest son Martin Ray was my grandfather, who would later become the father of my father John Frederick Cairney Rae.

CHAPTER 2

MY FATHER AND HIS STORY

Where should I try to begin my story about this man, my father, John Frederick Cairney Rae? As you can see my fathers name was a long distinguished sounding name. Three forenames were very impressive for 1911. Two of his names I can trace back to the Ray family and Cairney was his mother Rose Ann's maiden name. Most of his siblings had at least two names and most of those names had been used in the Ray/Rae family through many generations as far back as 1800[7]. They include boys names like James, John, Martin, Michael, William and Thomas and Catherine, Elizabeth and Margaret for the girls.

All of this once again brings me to the decision to write this story. How do I tell this story, who will be interested in my reasons for telling it and the journey I have taken over several years to fit together all the pieces of this puzzle? To put all the information I have discovered into writing is a daunting task but I agree there is a story out there and perhaps it needs to be told.

In many ways, like most of us, I waited too long to begin this journey. Older family members are no longer with us to ask. I also forget that I am getting older and if these events are not written down and recorded then they will be lost forever.

None of this would have been possible without a special meeting I had with my Aunt Margaret in the mid 1980s. The visit we shared that day was to be the trigger for all of this.

What passed between us that day concentrated all the longings I had to resolve issues from my childhood and to really begin my search for my father. Little did I realize that over thirty years later there are still some unanswered questions?

Margaret, my father's younger sister and I were always close. She in many ways had been a second mother to me when I was small. I always made sure to visit her when I went back to the UK, but this visit was really special. We had been sitting talking about her life growing up as the only girl in a family of boys and she was sharing her thoughts about her brother John, my dad, on one of my visits. Out of the blue she suddenly got up and went to her writing bureau and came back with a box of letters and photographs. She had kept all the letters her brother John had written to her while he was away from home serving in the Royal Air Force Volunteer Reserve during WW2. Many of his letters were censored but they were all beautifully written. Among her collection there were official letters from the British War Commission stating he was missing, letters telling of his death and where he was buried. There was a small box of the medals he had been awarded and photographs, precious photographs. I remember sitting with her, this very special lady, and pouring through all of this as we cried together. In a gesture of complete selflessness she handed me the box and said "this is for you, John was my brother but he was also your dad". This kind act cemented what was already a very special bond that the two of us shared. In all my years throughout my life when I was growing up, when I married and was raising my girls and even later when I moved so far away to America she was always there caring for me until the sad day when her letters stopped and she was no longer able to remember me. She died peacefully in 2008 and I still miss her.

At that moment when I was given this treasured gift I decided "I have to do something with this I can't just put this away." Thus began my mission to find out about this man and the Rae family to which I belonged.

It became my version of a mid-life crisis. I didn't go out and buy a fast sports car or take a world cruise. I always get seasick on boats. I just set myself the task of being the family historian uncovering, as I have recorded, my Rae roots with no idea where it would lead me. It was and still is an interesting journey as there had always been something or maybe some-one missing. I think most of all I wanted to know more about "this person in the pictures with the wonderful name." When I looked through the photographs of my dad John Rae I began to wonder who he had been. He was obviously some-one much loved by his younger sister who spoke about with such love and affection. Of course I had heard my mother speak lovingly of him especially as she tried to choose the inscription for his headstone for his grave so far away in a coun-try called Poland, someone she too still loved very much. Despite the memories of the two women I loved best in the world I still did not feel I knew John Frederick Cairney Rae.

As I read and reread the letters he had written to his sister so long ago, I began to get a better picture of my dad. They were full of the general day to day happenings of life during those dark days. He was making sure all the people he knew were OK and he was missing everyone and just the everyday pleasures of peacetime and being at home. Although he was far from home he sounded content, he enjoyed the small things like newspapers his brother Tommy sent or a new pen he had been given. His letters were also about his wife and new baby daughter Rosemary. He was concerned about how they were and hoped Margaret and her husband Charlie would be able to visit them. He sounded so proud. He always signed his letters "Your loving brother John F.C. or Bro John FC". Many of these letters were censored to make sure that he was not telling people where he was or of what he was doing. A letter he wrote on July 27, 1944 was again positive. He had received photos of me and declared "the baby does look fine" and he continues "the war is finally getting near finished.

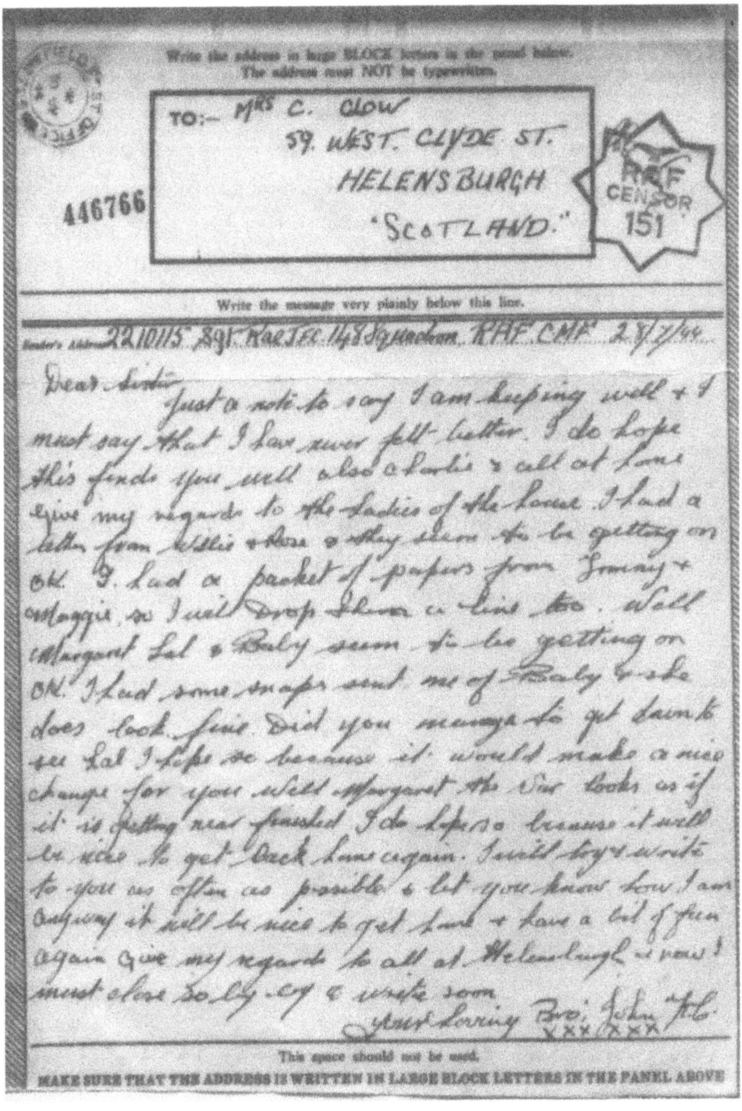

Write the address in large BLOCK letters in the panel below.
The address must NOT be typewritten.

446766

TO:– Mrs C. CLOW
59. WEST. CLYDE ST.
HELENSBURGH
"SCOTLAND."

RAF CENSOR 151

Write the message very plainly below this line.

Sender's Address 2210115 Sgt Rae J.C. 148 Squadron RAF. CMF 28/7/44

Dear Sister
Just a note to say I am keeping well & I must say that I have never felt better. I do hope this finds you well also Charlie & all at home give my regards to the ladies of the house. I had a letter from Willie & Rose & they seem to be getting on OK. I had a packet of papers from Jimmy & Maggie so I will drop them a line too. Well Margaret Lal & Baby seem to be getting on OK. I had some snaps sent me of Baby & she does look fine. Did you manage to get down to see Lal I hope so because it would make a nice change for you. Well Margaret the War looks as if it is getting near finished I do hope so because it will be nice to get back home again. I will try & write to you as often as possible & let you know how I am. Anyway it will be nice to get home & have a bit of fun again. Give my regards to all at Helensburgh & now I must close so bye-bye & write soon.

Your loving Bro: John XX
XXX XXX

This space should not be used.
MAKE SURE THAT THE ADDRESS IS WRITTEN IN LARGE BLOCK LETTERS IN THE PANEL ABOVE

Last letter from John Rae written to his sister Margaret

I do hope so because it will be nice to get back home again and have a bit of fun".

This was to be the last letter Margaret received as a week later his plane was shot down over Poland and he did not survive.

He was the man in the pictures that Margaret showed me, the man with the wonderful name. He was my dad but also a man I did not know and as my searches began to unfold his story, he is the one I came to admire and become very proud to be a part of.

MORE FAMILY HISTORY

My grandfather Martin Rae, the youngest son of Michael and Catherine Rae was born in Kamptee, Madras, India in on 30th September, 1872. He was employed as a Ships Plater in the Clyde Shipyards. Rose Ann Cairney, his wife, was born 1874

Rae Family c 1922.

and came from Lugar in Ayrshire was the daughter of Andrew and Margaret Cairney where her father was a Furnace Labourer. They were married at St Francis Roman Catholic Church in Glasgow on July 15, 1895. They settled down to married life in Govan raising a large family. My father was born on February 17, 1911 sharing the same birthday as his oldest brother Michael, fifteen years his senior, who was born in 1896. At the time of his birth his brothers were considerably older and most of them had left school. At that time I believe the school leaving age was 12 or 13. John was the sixth son born to Martin and Rose Ann Rae then of 6 Dunn Street, Dalmuir near Glasgow, Scotland.

Later in 1914 his sister Margaret and in 1920 a younger brother Francis were born. By the time the youngest brother was born my dad was nine and the oldest boys were so much older that my Aunt Margaret told me "they felt more like uncles than brothers."

Tracing my father's early life was not easy but I do know that most of his family worked in the large shipyards on the River Clyde. This at one time was virtually a one industry area and the mainstay of employment and of course was the heyday of ocean going liners built in shipyards like John Brown. The luxury liners like the Queen Mary and Queen Elizabeth were built here. My grandfather Martin worked at John Browns Shipyard and managed to get his sons "set on" as it was called. The oldest son Martin was a shipwright, his brother Michael became an electrician and Andrew and James were employed as boilermakers.

Martin and Rose Ann had eight children in all. Apart from Thomas who was the oldest, all the oldest brothers Andrew, Michael, Martin, and William immigrated to the United States of America during the late 1920's and early 30's, settling in New Jersey or Vermont. This they had done by one brother making the long sea journey, settling in America and finding work and having done so sent for another brother. This process was repeated and I have been told that it was planned that eventually all the family would make their way to America. The younger siblings who remained in Scotland became a very close knit group. My dad and his sister Margaret were very close as was their youngest brother Francis (Frank). They were special people who I treasured and who would help me in the years to follow when tragic circumstances happened to both my aunt and later to me.

I did find on some of my searches that John Rae was in the Merchant Navy[8] for a short period of time between January and May 1934. His reason for leaving is unknown at this time of writing. Maybe like me he was not a "good sailor." I can find virtually no details about his life between 1934 and 1939.

Alice Johnson my mother date unknown.

I am not sure why my dad moved away from his home in Scotland but he appears to have found employment working in and living in the Hammersmith area in London as a fitters mate. It was here that he met my mother Alice Johnson. She was known affectionately by everyone as Lal.

My mother was born at No 18, Second Row in the village of Ellington, Northumberland to Thomas and Mary Elizabeth Johnson on April 26, 1914.[9] Ellington Pit was one of the many coal mining communities in the North East corner of England. My grandfather Thomas Johnson was a miner[10] and had recently been promoted to the position of Deputy and moved with his family to a new house owned by the mining company in Ellington village

My mum like my dad had grown up in a large family. Her mother had a busy and hard life as a miner's wife. Her two oldest sons Tom and Harry like their father were miners and they were all working different shifts. This meant that my grandmother was kept constantly busy preparing meals, washing dirty pit clothes and preparing their bait boxes (meals to take down the pit) and of course making sure she had kettles of hot water for their baths when the arrived home from their shift. With his new job my grandfather had a raise in pay but it came with added responsibility. My mother Alice and her elder sister Annie of course had to help with the household duties when they were at home. The house had a large garden where my grandfather grew vegetables and raised chickens. He also had an allotment for further production of vegetables and where he also raised pigs.

The girls were responsible to collect the eggs from the henhouse. This was a job my mother hated because my grandfather also kept a horse called Bobby which he used to pull his cart around the villages selling fish. He was a resourceful man and did what ever he could to make some extra money for the family. My mother's eldest sister whom I called Nana told me a tale of my mother going to collect the eggs from the hen house and being trapped there by Bobby the horse who was known to have a mean streak. Of course Nana had no fear of the horse and used to ride him bareback and could not understand my mothers fear. Samuel my mother's younger brother continued the tale by telling me that they suddenly realized that my mother was missing when the table had been set for their meal and my mum did not appear. They went looking for her and

Samuel Johnson age 10. Photo courtesy of Tom Johnson his son.

eventually found her in tears stuck in the henhouse looking quite a sight.

From the stories I have been told the younger members of the Johnson family seemed to have had lots of fun as they grew up. My Uncle Sam was the joker in the family. When we sat down to talk he told me, in his wonderful "Geordie accent" (the dialect of the people who lived in Northumberland spoke) many stories about he and my mum. Of the time when she had spent cleaning the back yard and he came walking through in his "clarty boots" (muddy boots) and she had to clean the yard again. He said she was quite angry with him but when he pulled a silly face she couldn't manage to keep a straight face and they both ended up laughing and he set to and helped her clean the mess he had made. There was the time when he had been very ill and missed a lot of school and my mum spent time with him helping him catch up on his lessons so he wouldn't be behind when he returned to school. He said he had never forgotten that kindness. Even at this early age she was a caring person and she never seemed to loose that special quality.

Life was hard and there were not many opportunities for work where she lived so my mother, like my father, had moved away from her home traveling to the south of England to find work. She settled in Carshalton and took a job as a ladies maid. Later when her mother came for a holiday my mother showed her a house by the park. It had indoor plumbing and running water. My grandmother was amazed at these wonderful conveniences. She was still living in a coal mining village with a husband and sons "down the pit." It was a hard life in every way and certainly there were no indoor facilities. It was a tin tub in front of the fire with water heated on the stove and a walk down the yard to the privy. This formidable lady soon arranged for the family to move south to Surrey in the hopes of an easier life.

According to my mothers younger brother Sam my mother loved to dance. She and her friends would often travel up to London and go dancing at the Lyceum at the Strand or maybe at the Hammersmith Palais. He told me that is where he thought she met my dad. They saw each other often and eventually my dad asked her to marry him. At his time my mother was still "in service" and the standards she acquired then stayed with her. She was a wonderful home maker and took care of me and our home under some quite difficult circumstances.

John and Alice Rae Wedding Day, April 1938.

After the banns had been read my parents John and Alice were married at the Parish Church in Carshalton on April 18, 1938. The picture I have of them shows them standing outside The Church of All Saints looking very happy. When I finally was able to obtain a copy of my parent's marriage certificate I found a name I knew very well, that of Samuel Johnson who on reading the document more closely had been asked by my dad asked to be his best man. My Uncle Sam had never mentioned that when we had talked about my mum and dad.

My parents settled down to married life in Carshalton. Life went on but there loomed a possibility of war with Germany. The newspaper reports of the time were full of articles about the pending war. The British Government had given a guarantee to the Polish people on March 31, 1939 that Britain would support them if Poland where to be attacked by Germany. So only after a few months of marriage by September life as they knew it would begin to change.

CHAPTER 3

DECLARATION OF WAR

In 1938 Hitler had begun an expansion plan in order to provide "living space" for the German population. Austria had been annexed; the Sudetenland was next followed by Czechoslovakia in 1939. All of this was accomplished without any hostilities and so it was hoped that the invasion of Poland would be as simple. In the spring of 1939 Hitler had already begun making his plans to tackle the problem of Poland. He ordered his High Commissioner of the Armed Forces to start preparing his plan which had the code name "Fall Weiss" or "Plan White."[11] This name was used among the German officials and it would set into motion the plan to invade Poland no later than September 1st, 1939. That date was an important one specially chosen so that the heavy armored equipment to be used would not become bogged down in the fall mud on the Polish roads. It was widely known that the roads in Poland at that time had not been well maintained and were in poor condition.

A nonaggression pack was signed by Germany with the Soviet Union on August 1939 and in a secure clause Germany and the Soviet Union would divide Poland between them. Hitler gave orders for the invasion to begin on August 25, 1939 but delayed the attack when he heard that Britain had told the Polish Government that it would fully support Poland. Poland began to mobilize troops but were persuade by Britain to postpone general mobilization until August 31 in a last ditch effort to prevent a war.

On August 31, 1939 Hitler ordered hostilities against Poland to begin. In a prelude to this he sent Nazi SS troops dressed in Polish uniforms to stage a phony invasion on Germany damaging several minor installations on the German side of the border. This Hitler used to begin the attack on Poland calling it "an unforgivable act of aggression", and so on September 1st 1939 the German attack on Poland began.

Hitler's officers in charge thought they could send in two powerful wings of the Wehrmacht[12] to crush the Polish armed forces and in doing so they would be able to capture Warsaw. Whilst the Wehrmacht were undertaking this task the Germans decided to also send a stronger army group to invade and push the Polish forces east to Lwov and to also attack Warsaw from the west and north. The German forces advanced at great speed. Even though the Polish armed forces had mobilized over one million men they were hopelessly outmatched.

The news reached Britain but the British Government did not declare war on September 1st, 1939. They were hoping to hear from Germany that Hitler had decided to withdraw from Poland once he realized that the Western Allies would stand together. The Allies had made an agreement to support Poland. When September 3rd dawned and a reply had not been received from Hitler the Prime Minister Neville Chamberlain decided he needed to speak to the British people. Families gathered around their wireless sets hoping to hear that war had been averted but instead at 11:00 am on 3rd September 1939 the message they heard was not good. They heard the Prime minister say,

"Germany has not responded to the ultimatum and as a consequence this country is now at war with Germany."

In many homes there was stunned silence and then the realization set in that life would not be the same for many years to come. Many families would suffer great losses and hardships. Even though war had been declared Britain and France at first did little to help Poland. Many accused them of waging a "phony war." It was not until Germany invaded Norway in April 1940 and the Low Countries of France in June 1941 that hostilities began to escalate. Hitler then attacked the Soviet Union and the non aggression pack between the two countries was broken and Germany seized Poland. The Polish Government and military leaders fled the country.

World War Two would last many years with a huge loss of civilian life as well as fighting forces. There were unspeakable atrocities to innocent people and the disruption of daily life for many. The war machine of Nazi Germany marched into countries, occupying them and often enslaving the people. At the beginning the Allies had promised to support Poland in its struggles against Germany but in fact it ended as a war to defeat Germany.

Only after long and bitter struggles did the tragedy of the Polish people plight become clear. Poland's occupation was particularly harsh. They had fought so hard and won the war but still they had lost. Despite the Poles heroism, despite their important role in the winning coalition, they would not regain their independence for another fifty years.

When the war began England and its armed forces were not well prepared. The RAF and RAFVR Bomber Command were ill prepared. It consisted of twenty-three squadrons and two hundred and eighty aging planes!

As I sat and read the history books of these forces I began to wonder if large Army and Royal Air Force units had been ready in August 1939, when the war was first declared would Britain have be able to stand and defend Poland? If it had been ready for action and well equipped and aircrews trained and well funded and ready to invade with the allied armies the moment German forces crossed the Polish border, would the outcome have been very different? I am sure that question has been asked and answered many times.

Hitler and his German forces gradually marched their way across Europe with its forces sitting just across the English Channel waiting for the day they could invade England. I am convinced that they did not take into consideration the resolve and determination of the British people and her Empire that with their ground and air forces they could and would defeat Hitler.

Now that Britain was at war life became harder. Heavy bombing raids occurred on a nightly basis with the targets being large industrial areas of the country. Hitler's aim was to cripple the factories and prevent much needed war supplies being produced. Children were evacuated out of the cities to the more rural areas away from bombing targets and those adults, who were able, moved to less vulnerable locations.

My family which included my grandparents and my mother's sister her husband and young son plus my parents were still living in the south of England at the outbreak of war. They suffered the nightly bombing until finally they were able to move north away from the bombing and its disruption. My maternal grandfather had a twin sister Alice who lived in Morecambe, a seaside town on the North West coast of England, so with her help they all settled in to 202, Heysham Road, Morecambe. At that time most foodstuffs were being rationed and families had to register with local merchants such as butchers, milkmen. Those were the days when milk was delivered to your doorstep. It was not an easy move but my great-aunt was able to get then registered. They were glad to be away from the bombing and finally were happy to settle into a more peaceful life.

Alice, Grandma, and airmen billeted at "202."
Photo courtesy of Tom Johnson.

Like many families they wanted to be able to help in some way with the "War Effort[13]". The armed services were asking people to offer accommodation to the many service men and women. Many of the bases for these men and women did not have enough space to house everyone so they lived or as it was called "billeted"[14] with families in the local communities were they were stationed. So "202" as it affectionately became known was a hive of activity with the comings and goings of airmen. My dad's younger brother Frank was a Merchant Seaman on the North Atlantic Route and found himself ferrying much needed supplies by sea from America to Liverpool. He often came to stay when he was on leave. His sister Margaret's husband Charlie was also in the Army. My mother's younger brother Sam enlisted with the army and after all his training was shipped overseas with his unit in the

British Army fighting in Burma and India. Later in May of 1943 my dad finally received his papers to report to begin his basic training with the Royal Air Force Volunteer Reserve. There would eventually be four family members away from home fighting for their country

Nevertheless life went on, people made the best of a very bad situation. The women in the house kept busy with the everyday running of the house making sure that they were able to get the basic necessities with their ration cards. [15] Every one had a job to do and they kept busy.

The Army, Navy and Air Force prepared for action. Now with a war looming on the horizon the young men began to realize that they would in all probability find themselves becoming part of the armed forces. The men who were already serving in the three branches of the armed force's, the Royal Navy, Army and the youngest force the Royal Air Force were of course the first to be called up and leave their civilian jobs and rejoin their regiments and be assigned to their units. Lords Cricket Ground in London became the staging post for many of the young airmen until airfields and accommodations could be quickly built. The cost of building the long runways needed for the heavy bombers which were eventually being built cost a staggering £78,000 each.

Many of the first groups of volunteers were like many of the young men who had volunteered during the First World War expecting like their predecessors they would miss all the adventure. These young men some even younger that the enlistment age of eighteen, thought it would all likely be "over by Christmas" Some of these men also realized that if this was going to be a long war eventually young men like themselves would be called up and felt they may have a better say in their choice of where they would serve. There was at this time in Britain a great deal of unemployment and the Armed Services

offered "bed and board" and a wage however small. For many it was a better life than life on the dole.

This story concerns the men who became part of the Royal Air Force Volunteer Reserve. This was an all volunteer force formed in 1936 to provide support to the Royal Auxiliary Air Force formed in 1925. Initially the RAFVR was run by contractors who were employed by the Reserve Flying Schools as instructor members of the RAF or Reserve Air Force. Officers who completed a four year service were commissioned as pilots in the RAF. Navigation instructors were former master mariners without any flying or air experience.

The new recruits in the Royal Air Force Volunteer Reserve, (RAFVR) were men aged 18 to 25 who had completed part time training as Pilots, Observers and Wireless Operators. The plan was to have a reserve aircrew for use in the event of war but sadly these airmen were often viewed as "common people and not the right sort" to become officers. In 1939 the Royal Air Force (RAF) as it was known was staffed mainly by the Public School Club "Old Etonians and aristocrats" who saw it mainly as their "Private Club."

When war broke out the Air Ministry employed the airmen who served in the RAFVR as the aircrew to serve with the RAF. Notice that there seem to be two parts of the RAF. There was still somewhat of a class distinction. If you had attended the right public schools, Oxbridge and later Cranfield you became an officer in the RAF. Public school is a term used in Britain being a euphemism for private and extremely expensive school such as Eton or Rugby. At the beginning of the war this was probably true of all the Officer Class in all the armed forces. This certainly was not the place for the boys from the Local Authority schools or redbrick universities. These bright, often brighter boys became part of the RAFVR. Selection was done by checking the enlistee's background and the enlistee had no say in the matter.

Ironically when war was declared slowly things began to change. It then became possible for the Upper Classes in the RAF to be trained as navigators and find themselves under the command of a lad from the London Dockland who had been able to train as a Pilot W/O from the RAFVR. Still the divide was then and is still to this day somewhat noticeable in society of a "them and us" syndrome.

By 1939 the RAFVR had 6642 Pilots, 1625 Observers and 1946 Wireless Operators.

A civilian volunteer after he was accepted for aircrew training took the Oath of Allegiance and was then part of the RAFVR. Normally he returned to his civilian job until he was called for training. He was given a small silver lapel badge with his service number to show he had volunteered. Often this badge helped the men who were not yet in uniform from being harassed by the population who thought they were "not doing their bit" as it was called.

By 1941 more than half of Bomber Command was part of RAFVR. Most of the pre-war members now held commissions, and became Flight and Squadron commanders.

Over 125,000 men volunteered to serve in the RAFVR, Bomber Command. Over 55,573 lost their lives.

My dad John Rae chose to volunteer with the Royal Air Force Volunteer Reserve and I am told he wore his badge proudly. I have my own version about his reason for enlisting in the RAFVR. I have no knowledge that this is correct because I do not have anyone to ask. Because he was older than the average age of recruits which was 18 to 20 years, he may have thought that he could become a member of the Ground Crew who maintained the aircraft which was a much safer prospect than flying as the rear gunner which was what he eventually became.

When my dad did finally did get "the call" to report in May 1943.[16] He was 32 years old!

REPORTING FOR DUTY:

At the age of 32 when he reported my father was probably quite a bit older than the average recruit. Most of the information which was recorded and which we hear and read seem to tell us that the RAF was made up mainly of very young men but this was not always so. John Rae at the age of 32 was classed as NE (non exempt) on his records which meant that he was not employed in a job that the government thought was vital to the country or war effort so he had no choice but to report. I have no personal accounts of my fathers reporting to begin his service with the Royal Air Force in May of 1943 but have used his service records to follow his progress from his day of joining until his final flight on August 4/5 1944. One year and seventy eight days later.

No 3 Aircrew Recruiting Center, RAF Padgate.

When my father received orders to begin his service he first reported to Air Crew Selection Board (ACSB) at RAF Padgate in the north of England on May 17, 1943. He progressed very quickly into the training system as only three days later reported to NO 3 Recruiting Center which is the Royal Air Force Receiving Center again at Padgate near Warrington, not too far from his home in Morecambe. Like all recruits he spent several days undergoing thorough medical tests and from checking his service records he passed with Grade 1.

He was given written tests in a variety of subjects such as Math and English with a given set time for each set subject and the usual initial "square bashing."

He may have been sent to No 1 Air Crew Reception Center at St Johns Wood London and probably further training and the inevitable "square bashing."

Lastly he was subjected to a final interview with the Selection Board, and it was than he was assigned as an Aircraft Hand which was a Non Commissioned Officer posting and was "recommended for training as Air Gunner." Sadly he was not selected for Ground Crew. Once he had completed his initial interview he was "kitted out." This was the term used for supplying the new recruit with everything he needed for his day to day living as a member of the Royal Air Force from his uniform to toiletries plus kit bag to pack them all in. My dad John then passed on June 19, 1943 to 14 ITW which was the Initial Training Wing which I believe was based in the Yorkshire seaside resort of Bridlington and then followed Air Gunners training. Here he learned the various types of guns he might find himself using on operations. There was always inevitable drill undertaken along the promenade and open spaces of the town. He spent less than a month at Bridlington before he was on the move once more on July 31st, 1943. John Rae then began further more extensive training at the newly opened 12 AGS Air

John Rae West End Pier, Morecambe

Gunner School at RAF Bishops Court in Ireland. He was one of the first groups to attend this newly opened facility.

Here he began weeks of training first on ground based systems and then as he progressed he moved on to air firing practices from Ansons[17] against targets towed by Martinets.[18] During the early stages of the war gunners had served a duel role of wireless operators/ gunners but later these had become separated each becoming a separate trade. He completed training in seven weeks and qualified as an air gunner.

It was demanding few weeks learning how to operate the gun turrets and their machine guns which was complex. This training would eventually lead to a posting. Here he received the practical experience of operating the turret under flying conditions. Smaller bombers like the Armstrong Whitworth often called the "Whitley" were used for this training. Mock attacks were practiced until the air gunners became proficient. I can't imagine being in this tiny back turret while the plane is moving in all directions trying to avoid the attacking planes. It must have been like a roller coaster ride or perhaps worse.

At the end of the course final examinations were taken. He passed his final exams on 18th September 1943. John Rae was awarded his flying badge, his air gunner wings, and sergeant's stripes on the same day plus an increase in pay!

CHAPTER 4

AIR GUNNERS

Air Gunner Turret. Photo courtesy of David Birrell, Bomber Command Museum of Canada.

The pilots are the glamour boys
but ask them who has the tough
job in battle and they'll say

"It's the little guy in the back seat"

Author Unknown

The air gunner's job as part of the aircrew on operation flights was one of the loneliest places in the aircraft especially on the long night flights which the crews flying special duties flights endured.

While the other crew-members enjoyed some comfort from being near the rest of their team in the front part of the aircraft, Clifford Aspinall who was the airman who had the job as the mid-upper gunner spent the missions suspended on a canvas sling seat, his lower body in the draughty fuselage and his head and shoulders in the Plexiglas dome. I believe that he later volunteered to become a dispatcher responsible for getting the load of supplies out of the plane at the drop zone to be picked up by the partisans. The duty would make the long flights for him a little more bearable.

John Rae the rear gunner was not so lucky. He was confined to his tiny turret at the end of the fuselage and further away from his fellow crewmates and any heating system which often was sporadic. The rear turret was suspended in space at the extreme end of the fuselage; "Arse-end Charlie" as these gunners were often called had to cope with to the most violent movements of the aircraft. He was squeezed into the cramped metal and Perspex cupola with so little leg space that he had to place his flying boots into the turret before climbing in. At 5ft 7inches he was probably one the shortest members of the crew but when I looked again at a photo of my dad John Rae and Clifford Aspinall, Aspinall seemed even shorter then my dad. Many rear gunners removed a section of the Plexiglas to improve their view, and with temperatures at 20,000 feet reaching -40 degrees, frostbite was a regular occurrence. Through the entire flight over enemy territory, the rear gunner always knew that the Luftwaffe fighter pilots would, if they had a choice, attack from the rear and from underneath the bomber, so he was often first in line for elimination. During World War II 20,000 air gunners were killed while serving with Bomber Command.

Often when the crew was flying an operational mission, the only sounds John Rae would hear, apart from the constant deafening roar of the engines, would be the hiss of the oxygen and the occasional crackling, of the distorted voices of his crewmates in his earphones. From take off to landing on many flights, at times for over twelve hours, the air gunners were constantly rotating the turrets, scanning the surrounding blackness, quarter by quarter, for the gray shadow that could instantly become an attacking enemy night fighter. The air gunner's closest friends were likely his crewmembers in the forward section of the bomber and the relaxation of his vigilance for even a moment could mean death for them all.

It seems odd to me that the main role of my dad, the rear gunner, was not to shoot down enemy aircraft but it was to be the role of a lookout to warn his pilot of enemy planes. It is as if he was the human equivalent of "an early warning device." He would spend hours staring into the blackness of the night sky, but instead of an alarm sounding when an enemy plane approached he would shout into the intercom, the recognized term which all crew members were familiar, "Corkscrew port now!" and they all instinctively knew they were in for a bumpy ride. These words would have the pilot instantly begin a series of violent evasive maneuvers, throwing the heavy bomber around the sky with the crew hanging on for dear life! It was not a pleasant term to use as my dad would have the worst seat in the plane during this maneuver. Usually if an enemy fighter pilot knew he had been seen, he would not try to follow the bomber through its twists and turns. Instead he would simply look for another aircraft, hoping that it might have a less alert air gunner. Many air gunners would often complete their tour of operations without firing a single shot "in anger," but the stress they were constantly under was equal to those, who, with guns ablaze in the night, became part of brief, terrifying, life and death battle in the night with enemy aircraft which were much faster and able to move about the sky so much more easily then the heavy bombers such as the Halifax.

At the beginning of the war there were airmen in an aircrew who had two jobs rolled into one. They were known as Wireless Operator/Air Gunner and were responsible for radio operations as well as the operation of the gun turret. Later, when the larger four-engine bombers which had a crew of seven came into service this combined role was no longer necessary

**Air Gunner in Rear Turret. Photo courtesy of
David Birrell, Bomber Command Museum
of Canada.**

AIR GUNNER TACTICS

Information from a Gunnery Course Manual used at
No 2 Bombing and Gunnery School

Mossbank, Alberta Saskatchewan.

General Hints List for Air Gunners

- "Search sky before take off and landing, your a/c is most vulnerable.
- If gun fire, search for fighter; take evasive action.

- Always watch your own tail.
- Conserve your ammo; if you're fired upon from long range, instruct pilot to use evasive action.
- Never fly straight or dive when under attack.
- Use good team work with rest of crew.
- Patrol across the sun, never into or away from it.
- Never turn away from an attack, always towards.
- If using tracer at night, remember it tends to momentarily destroy your night vision; -hold your fire until necessary.
- If on reconnaissance aircraft; your job is to return with information; not to seek combat with enemy aircraft.
- Aim of enemy fighter is to destroy; aim of bomber air gunner is to get safely to target and back to base.
- Never fire until fired upon.
- All aircraft approaching are considered to be enemy until identified otherwise.
- REMEMBER: TO BE SURPRISED IS TO BE LOST .
- If your own guns fail or are damaged during an attack use your ingenuity to outwit the attacker."

It almost seemed that the gunners could copy this list and keep in safely in their uniform to refer to if needed but I am sure that in the heat of an attack they instinctively knew exactly the actions they need to take. Survival mode kicked in!

METHOD OF SEARCH

The courses at the Gunnery School they attended John Rae and Clifford Aspinall would give them the basic information on the use and general maintenance and the type of guns they would use. One of the courses which these new air crews attended was invaluable for the trainee gunners. It gave some idea of how easy it was for the enemy in their lighter fighter and of course much faster aircraft to approach the much slower heavy bombers and the instructors shared useful pieces of information with the new trainees. Often these instructors had finished their tours of duty or had in some cases been shot down and managed to return to England and had been assigned to become part of the training staff. The information they shared with the trainee gunners was therefore from first hand knowledge and most importantly experience. I am sure my dad and Clifford Aspinall, and all these attending the course, listened intently as the instructor offered the following advice to the gunners who listened carefully to first hand information from men who had most likely had to use some of the suggestions they were now offering to the novice airmen yet to see action.

The instructors would tell the men that "Jerry" especially when he was flying at night has a big bag of tricks for decoys.

"He will send one aircraft along your course with identification lights on and then send one behind you on your tail; or has one come out of the moon. If anything like this happens you should look and search on the opposite side of your aircraft for the real attacker. Jerry has a favorite position, if he can get it. It is to come from below and climb up to 300 yards from you, directly underneath your aircraft then stall his aircraft and hit your fuselage with machine-gun and cannon fire. If this happens the bombs being carried explode and the bomber disintegrates. So every now and then you need to communicate with your pilot and have him do steep turns so you can search below the aircraft for fighters."

Instructors would add:

"Searchlights on the ground often co-operate with the fighters in many different ways. Sometimes they send a series of dots in your direction. Sometimes they wave along your course. If this happens and they suddenly go off, then you know a fighter has found you. If there is cloud cover below, the searchlights light up the clouds and you are silhouetted for the fighter which will be flying above you."

Jerry also uses what we called:

"Chandelier flares." This is either a single large flare or a group of 3 - 5 flares. They are shot from the ground and hang in the air for a long time at your level. They light up everything for miles around and show your position to the fighter."

One of the most important things to remember they were told is:

"Jerry loves a sleeping target. If he does find you and he knows you have spotted him there he will, nine times out of ten, go away and find another bomber whose gunner is not so alert."

Lastly the course would end by the instructor offering a final piece of advice telling the gunners:

"You are there as an Air Gunner whose first job is to protect your bomber and crew mates and not to shoot down fighters."

The following Golden Rule that was stressed on many occasions by the instructors was:

"Never fire unless it is necessary. Always take evasive action. Firing gives your position away to every night fighter in that vicinity."

David Birrall, Director of Library/Archives/Displays from the Bomber Command Museum of Canada, Nanton, Alberta, Canada kindly gave me permission to use information about Air Gunner Training held by the museum.

CHAPTER 5

BECOMING A CREW

Having completed his trade training the next step my dad, John Rae, took was joining other airmen and becoming a crew prior to beginning operations and so it was that he was posted to 18 Operational Training Unit (OTU) at RAF Finningly, Yorkshire on September 19, 1943. Here the new aircrews would spend at least five weeks of intensive training. This was the unit where he would meet and fly with four other airmen he would eventually "be posted" with on operations. This system was called "crewing up" and it was a very simple procedure. The men were assembled in a hanger and told to form crews. It was at this point that the pilots started looking for suitable airmen to form their crew at the beginning of this course. They were often unknown to each other but generally were allowed to make up their own crews. There was no interference from "the powers that be". These men chose who they were going to fly with and once a crew was formed they flew each mission together and became an efficient, effective team relying on each other. The captain or "skipper" as he was often affectionately called usually had the final say.

In that same group of airmen was then Flying Officer James Girvan McCall RAFVR who was beginning his second tour and had been appointed to a commission on August 5th 1942[19] from the rank of sergeant. He was from Edinburgh. Among the other aircrew there was of course Sergeant Robert Peterson RCAF the bomb aimer and Flying Officer Phillip James Anderson RCAF navigator both from Canada, and Sergeant

Alan Jolly RAFVR the wireless operator from Fleetwood and my dad Sergeant John Frederick Cairney Rae RAFVR.

I have a letter written by my dad on September 22, 1943[20] to his sister Margaret in Helensburgh, Scotland. He was ill with flu and he describe the base as "damp and miserable" he sounded tired and yet he assured her 'but we have a good mess to sit in so we are not too badly off." He was still finishing off the course but was very worried about his wife Lal who was in the hospital. She was pregnant and had been ill for some time.

Now the real training began. It was important for each crew member to do his designated task to the best of his ability for his own satisfaction and for the well being of the rest of the crew.

Practices were at a nearby bombing range, then cross country flying, night flying, all the time the crew was building their trust in each other and their "Skipper". The training continued until they were completely confident.

In another letter to his sister Margaret he tells her that he flew over Helensburgh where she lived and said "I thought how near yet so far away I was."

The fact that they were sent to RAF Finningly probably influenced their future posting because while my dad and his crew were at 18 OTU RAF Finningly, (Operational Training Unit) Polish crews were also training. This was where the crews who would be sent to the Middle East[21] to undertake special duties over Poland and Eastern Europe were sent for their training. Ironically these same aircrews found themselves flying alongside 148 Special Duties Squadron in Brindisi, Italy to which the McCall crew would eventually find themselves posted.

Little is known of the exact training they underwent but records show that they, the McCall crew, were involved in a minor accident on December 2 1943 while they were practicing circuit training at Bircotes. For some reason the pilot McCall made a heavy landing in a Wellington X LN186 which was wrecked but luckily no one was hurt.

For the first few weeks my dad continued to receive advanced training in his own field as Air Gunner and the other airmen in the aircrew continued further training in their own fields. Pilots, Navigators, Bomb Aimers and Wireless Operators all had special training programs to make sure that they were proficient at their allotted position in an aircrew. They flew and trained together practicing various situations and became confident that they would be able to work as an independent team with no outside help if such a situation occurred. They were all individuals but they thought as one. On most occasions they flew the smaller bombers which had a crew of five and later when sent for training on the heavy bombers at the Heavy Conversion Unit (HCU) where they added a second gunner for the top turret and a flight engineer.

Now that my dad had met his fellow crew members and they had all completed their individual final extensive training, they decided that they would work well together. They perfected all that they had learned through hard work in their training and practice. At that time and from then on they were completely responsible and able to carry out the tasks to which they would be assigned. When they finished the course on 20 February 1944 these five airmen were then posted to No 11 base which was stationed at RAF Lindholme not too far from Finningly and still in the North of England.

This base was made up of three stations Lindholme, Blyton and Sandtoft. Each of these units was where the Heavy Conversion Units were stationed and where crews were sent to learn to operate the four- engine planes such as the Halifax or Lancaster. These stations were in fact controlled by Bomber

Command and the command to which most of the aircrews were eventually sent but at RAF Lindholme they also undertook the training of crews who were to become part of the overseas units of the air force. These "heavies" as they were called needed a crew of seven so the first task of the five McCall crew was to find an extra gunner and flight engineer. Sergeants Clifford Aspinall RAFVR who hailed from Blackpool was chosen as the Upper Gunner and Sergeant Charles Underwood RAFVR from Nasby, Yorkshire was to be the flight engineer. Training continued and at some stage having found that they worked well together and passed the tests they were put through by the training program they were then deemed fit to be passed on to the next and probable final stage before being sent off to their first posting for which they had been earmarked for service. Instead of being posted to a Bomber Command squadron they found themselves eventually moving to RAF Pershore in Worcestershire to train for an overseas unit deployment.

The crew was ready for operational flying. From then on they were now known as the McCall crew. These names now have a special part in this story.

They are:

Flt. Lt. James Girvan McCall RAFVR, Pilot from Edinburgh, Scotland.

F/O Phillip James Anderson RCAF, Navigator from Toronto, Canada.

Flt. Sgt. Robert Orlando Peterson, RCAF, Bomb Aimer from Revelstoke, B.C., Canada.

Sgt. Alan Jolly, RAFVR, W/Op Air Gunner from Fleetwood, England

Sgt. Walter Charles Underwood, RAFVR, Flt. Eng. from Nottingham England. He joined during the HCU training when the crew increased to seven airmen

Sgt. Clifford Aspinall, RAFVR, Air Gunner from Blackpool, England. He joined the crew when they began their training on the heavy bombers such as the Halifax

And Sgt. John Frederick Cairney Rae, RAFVR, and Rear Air Gunner he was originally from Dalmuir, Scotland, my dad.

Two Scotsmen, two Canadians, three from England, two of them "Lancashire lads."

From this time until the crew were posted to the Overseas Aircraft Dispatch Unit (OADU) their time could have been spent in three ways. Home leave which I am sure would have been very welcome and thoroughly enjoyed. They may have been sent to an Escape Course run by the army which would have taken over three weeks. This was never listed on airmen's Personal Official Record and finally the crew would complete their assignment to a Heavy Conversion Unit where they had learned to fly the bigger and more powerful Halifax.

On speaking with a veteran pilot, Larry Toft, of 148 Squadron he assured me that when he was going through all his training, he at no time felt that training or postings appeared rushed to get them to a Squadron although he does say that "figures since reveal there were frequent vacancies."

When airmen arrived at RAF Pershore they joined a course at NO 1 Ferry Unit where they received extra training in navigation and fuel conservation. This training would become invaluable on the many long flights they flew when they became part of 148 Special Duties Squadron. Some further practicing for further air testing of aircraft and circuits and bumps also called touch and goes followed. This training lasted a period of three weeks.

The McCall crew was posted on May 18, 1944 to No 2 Overseas Aircraft Dispatch Unit (OADU) at RAF St Mawgan which was the place were crews collected and air tested their brand new aircraft. This unit was connected to No 1 Ferry Unit at Pershore. They were allocated a Halifax for delivery to the Middle East and they would have spent the next few days preparing for the long flight before setting off on May 22, 1944. During that time the crew was placed back on the books of the NO 11 Base pending their arrival in North Africa at which time they were transferred to the establishment of No 2 Air Crew Reception Center (ACRC) at RAF Rabat Sale, Morocco, North Africa. Having made the long flight and successfully delivered their aircraft the McCall crew were transferred once again to No 1 Base Personal Depot in Italy to await their final posting to an operational unit at the beginning of June. It is difficult to determine the exact date of their arrival in Brindisi as the records are hand written and hard to read.

At some time prior to the McCall crews first posting they were given home leave.

CHAPTER 6

SPECIAL HOME LEAVE

The year was 1944.

The month was April.

The date was the 22nd which I believe was a Saturday.

The place was Queen Victoria Hospital, Morecambe, Lancashire..

That was the date I was born to Alice (Lal) and John Rae the day we became a family.

My dad was by then a Sergeant in the Royal Air Force Volunteer Reserve (an all volunteer force). He had been called up in May 1943 and had at this time completed most of his training,

John Rae had been given a pass for a few days special leave to be with my mother who had not been well. He was as I have been told, by his sister Margaret, "a very proud father" and reading his letters that statement has proved to be correct. He spent time with his wife Lal and me settling us into our home and making sure that my mum had the help she needed before he returned to finish the rest of his training at gunnery school.

On returning to his base he then began the process of becoming the rear gunner and part of the McCall crew. This would be his final training before joining his squadron.

A few weeks later prior to the McCall crew's first posting to an operational squadron they were once again given home leave. I am sure that my dad welcomed this break to be with his wife. He proudly went to register my birth on May 2nd and then on May 7, 1944 I was christened Rosemary Dawn at a simple ceremony at Saint Johns Church, in Heysham. The names that my parents had chosen for me were special. The Rose is in remembrance of my dad's mother Rose Ann Rae and the Mary is after my maternal grandmother Mary Elizabeth, hence Rosemary. It is a special name that was given to me with obviously a lot of thought by my parents. Church Records show that my christening ceremony on May 7th was shared with another family, the Lowe family of Morecambe who were their with their baby daughter Amy. Little did we realize that many years later Amy and I would meet again?

My Christening was a happy day, photos were taken of my family and me, of my dad, mum and I and my aunt and older cousin. Little did the family realize that these would be the first and only images taken of us as a family?

John Rae with his daughter
Rosemary, May 1944.

Alice & John Rae with their daughter
Rosemary May, 1944.

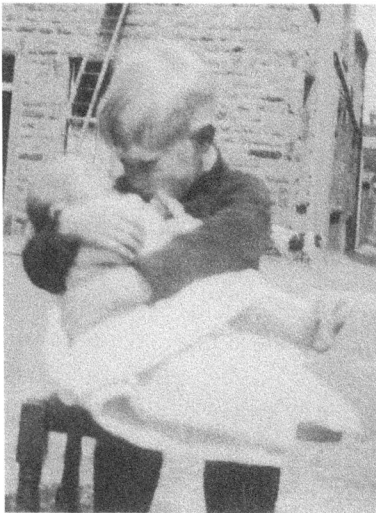

Cousin Ivan and
Rosemary May, 1944.

Alice Rae's sister Annie,
her son Ivan and
Rosemary May, 1944.

CHAPTER 7

THE MIGHTY HALIFAX

THE BUILDING OF HALIFAX JP 162FS-S for Sugar.

In a letter I received from Terry Marker of "Operations Dark of the Moon" he shared with me the information about the building of Halifax JP162FS s for sugar.

Halifax production, Park Royal. Photo courtesy of Terry Marker.

Halifax JP162 was built by the London Aircraft Production Group, (L.A.P.G.) which was a part of the London Public Transportation Board. This was the company that built the Red London buses in peacetime such as the famous Routemaster which has very recently been retired from service. The company was based in Leavensden, and Park Royal, near London. This aircraft was a "BII SOE (Special Operations Executive) and it was built specially for the supply, and agent drops that this group undertook. JP162 took to the air for the first time in September 1943, as part of a batch of several hundred aircraft, built to contract between July and September 1943. It was then delivered to No 3 Overseas Aircraft Preparation Unit, (OAPU) and was made ready for the Mediterranean Theatre of War. When ready, it was delivered to No 301 Ferry Transfer Unit, (301 FTU), where it was finally delivered to 148 Squadron. This aircraft was numbered JP 162 FS "S" for sugar and sent to replace the previous "S" aircraft, JP286-S, "S-Sugar" which had flown on Operation Savanna101/Deerhurst and had been lost a month earlier, on the ill fated night of 3/4th July, 1944 where four aircraft were lost.

Like my Father, his aircraft had a similarly short career. The payload on most of the flights it made to aide the partisans in Northern Italy, Yugoslavia and Poland would have been arms, food, clothing, and money, to support the partisans and the Poles in their fight in the Warsaw Uprising. The Polish people hold all of our lost aircrew in great respect for their efforts.

Halifax JP 162 FS finally became part of 148 Squadron. On July 19 1944, Flt. Lt. James McCall and his crew had ferried the aircraft from No 144 Maintenance Unit in Maison Blanche, North Africa to their squadron base in Brindisi. This aircraft would eventually be the plane that this crew flew the most in their missions and of course it was the aircraft which would fail to return (FTR) from the Polish mission on August 4/5 1944 which the McCall crew was flying. Ironically JP162-S had replaced JP 286–S which had crashed a month earlier. Circumstances are eerily similar; four aircraft lost on both the mission in July and one month later on the August mission.

AIRCREW STATIONS ON THE HALIFAX

The Halifax was classed as a Heavy Bomber and was operational with an aircrew of seven. Each of the seven assigned airmen had their own "crew stations" on the aircraft and everyone continually searched the sky for enemy aircraft. On a general note, all aircrew received flying pay, which was approximately an extra 20 pence a day in today's money.

Halifax Cockpit. Photo courtesy of Larry Toft.

Cockpit Pilot and Flight Engineer:

Most heavy bombers had only one pilot as was the case of the Halifax. The pilot sat on the left side. The controls were heavy so when the crew was sent out on the long flights it must have been exhausting job for the pilot. The center and right panels were made up with engine instruments. The navigation and bombing aides were added to as new developments were made in those fields. There was a fold down seat on the right hand side of the pilot which the flight engineer used. The throttles were in the center which both these men could reach. When they were taking off the flight engineer handled the throttles while the pilot kept the airplane straight. The flight engineers job was to help the pilot. He continually monitored all the instruments and the fuel gauges and the engines and if necessary kept the airplane balanced by transferring fuel. Both these crew members worked as a team to keep the airplane flying safely.

I was told by a veteran pilot from 148 Squadron.

"Pilot training had been thorough with no corners cut so when it came time to convert to flying the heavy bombers like the four engine Halifax it began by getting familiar with the cockpit controls. This was done by being blindfolded. The instructor gave a briefing on take off speeds and rate of climb and then expected the pilot to be able to fly the aircraft. He sat beside the pilot on a fold up seat but had no controls but could give advice as needed. Landings were also demonstrated once and then the trainee followed this by three half hour sessions with the instructor still sitting in the fold up seat practicing take-off and landings. These sessions were short because the physical effort was so demanding. After all this the pilot who was converting to these large airplanes did a further three hours of solo circuits and bumps. Later came some training on flying with three or two engines in case of emergency. The total time spent on this training was ten hours dual and 23 hours solo."

The pilot now knew how to handle and fly this huge aircraft but at no time during his training was he ever given advice or have to attend lectures or classes on how to lead and be a good captain. That very important role was left to him.

Navigator Seat:

Halifax Navigator Station Photo Courtesy of Larry Toft.

The navigator had the job of finding the way to and from the target. He used instruments such as compass, alternator and air speed indicator to help him calculate where he was. He would be giving course corrections, turning points and timing to destination during the flight. Often these simple calculations were not enough to ensure that they were at the target and often targets were missed. Later when new more sophisticated instruments were available and with the introduction of the Path Finder Force used in some of the German Raids things improved. The Halifax's flying in the Special Duties Squadrons did not have this luxury. The men in these aircrews flew alone and had to rely on their own calculations which were vital to the success of a crew.

Bomb Aimer:

Halifax Bomb Aimer Station Photo courtesy of Larry Toft.

The bomb aimer on the Special Duties Squadrons had a slightly different role to than of his fellow bomb aimers who flew the flights to Germany. His task in these specially equipped Halifax planes was to advise the pilot on the run up to the dropping zones and to make sure that the supplies were being dropped. He also manned the front turret gun which in most cases in the Halifax was a Boulton Paul turret which was fitted into the nose of the aircraft.

Wireless Operator:

Halifax Wireless Operator Photo courtesy of Larry Toft.

In this crew station the airman who was assigned to this position was responsible for communication and conveyed the wind speeds to the navigator. Soon after take off the wireless operator had to manually unwind the 50ft + aerial which trailed below and behind the aircraft aided by a large lead weight on the end of the aerial. In flight he maintained a constant listening role of all radio messages universally being transmitted singling out and decoding any directed to his aircraft, perhaps a recall or divergence. Total radio silence precludes a reply, only emergency message near base were allowed, for example severe damage, need for ambulance or ditching coordinates. The wireless operator was bound to his radio set for entire flight only free to help dispatcher to push out packages at drop zone. It was also important that he remembered to reel in the aerial just before landing, for a detached lead weight could become a missile.

Mid Upper Turret:

The airman assigned to this crew station in the aircraft sat in a sling device with his legs dangling below and his head in the Perspex bubble in the middle of the aircraft. The guns in this turret were originally designed for day time use so were not much use in the Special Duties Squadrons which did much of their flying at night. The upper gunner, as was the rear gunner, was in fact the eyes of the pilot from above and behind. In some instances, such as the supply missions flown out of Brindisi Italy, these gunners were asked to volunteer to become the Dispatcher to take charge of dropping the containers and packages and sometimes agents when the aircraft reached its drop zone area. The gunner who volunteered had to do four practice jumps which were supervised by the U.S.A.F. They very rarely use their guns.

Rear Gunner Turret:

The loneliest and coldest crew station on the Halifax and the most dangerous one. It was a cramped compartment and gunners were often of small stature to be able to fit, so they often had to place their boots in the turret before climbing in. The gunners were in such a confined space which often got very cold and

Halifax Rear Gunner Station Photo courtesy of Larry Toft.

there was literally no room to move easily to keep their circulation as it should be. A combination of fear, tension and oxygen tended to make the gunners mouth very dry so for that reason they were issued with glucose sweets and chewing gum. Halifax aircraft were fitted with a variety of Boulton Paul turrets but the rear gunner was the main defense of the Halifax. He had an important but dangerous roll. In many cases the rear gunner aided the pilot and dispatcher relaying the information that the supplies had been dropped successfully. Night fighters were prone to attack from the rear and so the rear gunner was the most venerable and in the direct line of fire. In order to have better vision many gunners often removed the Perspex panel but this would leave them in unbelievable cold and they often suffered frostbite. An alert rear gunner was often the airmen who saved his crew crying "Corkscrew starboard Go"

Dispatcher:

This position in the Halifax flown by the Special Duties Squadron was a member of the aircrew, usually one of the gunners, who were approached and asked to volunteer. If on deciding to volunteer, they were then sent on a special course and had to complete four jumps in parachute training. The dispatchers had to experience the jumps to know exactly how the parachute reacts and feels during a jump.

This is the personal account of Dave Lambert a veteran gunner of 148 Squadron who volunteered at the age of 19 for this dangerous position on the aircraft.

"I tied myself to the aircraft with a life line short enough to allow me to be connected at all times to my intercom. I never wore my parachute in place for good reasons. On the face of the parachute pack a D shaped steel release pin protruded slightly from an elasticized pocket, and if the pack was clamped in position, high on my chest, under my chin, it would impede my vision and with the added fearful risk of the D ring catching on something instantly releasing the 'chute."

He continues

"I spent the outward flight rearranging the packages which sometimes filled the width and almost the height of the interior around the trap doors. The Wireless Operator would on occasion assist."

Larry Toft the pilot and Dave Lambert's "skipper" on the Halifax says

"If we failed to make the drop then, on the return flight to base he informed me and would also inform us of what the packages contained, accept my invitation to sit beside me on the fold up 'dickey' seat, or make up for lost sleep."

The dispatcher was responsible for the care of Agents or "Joes" as they were often called attaching a static line to their parachute clear of his own feet, guiding them to their exit position, watching for the red/green light signals. At no time did he talk to the agents except to yell "good luck" as the left the plane all the time relying only on his calm professional attitude to reassure their usual nervous state.

The extra eighth crew member who was listed on some operation flights was usually a dispatcher to witness and learn more of this dangerous duty.

Aircrew drew a parachute and harness for each flight they undertook handing it back when they returned. If the airman's parachute was due to be re-hung and repacked, then the packer, usually a W.A.A.F, before accepting it would always insist that the airman pull the "D" ring to successfully release the chute which would prove to the airmen that the parachute would have in fact saved his life. There would be smiles all round and according to my 148 Squadron veteran source the crewman would insist that the young lady accept a monetary gift or, if not a kiss as a reward! This was a very serious ritual in every squadron.

All pictures and information of Halifax crew stations was kindly supplied by Larry Toft, Veteran pilot of 148 Special Duties Squadron.

CHAPTER 8

ABOUT THE Mc CALL CREW

The Airmen of Halifax JP162FS-S[22]

My dad John Rae was one of seven men who were part of this aircrafts crew who flew together on each mission. Each airman was assigned to a Crew Station which they had spent many hours training for but they were often able to help each other if it became necessary.

We here much about "how young these airmen were" and when I look at old photographs many of them look as though they should still been in school! The McCall crew was an older crew. I had thought that my dad was the oldest at 33 but the upper gunner Sgt. Aspinall was the oldest at 37. The Canadians F/O Anderson and Sgt. Peterson were 35 and 30 respectively. The young ones of the aircrew were the pilot Flt. Lt. McCall 23, Sgt. Jolly was 22 and the baby of the crew was Sgt. Underwood a mere 20 years old.

All these airmen are part of my story and they deserve to be recognized. They spent many hours together training and flying together on these long dangerous missions relying on each others skills to keep themselves safe. They also spent long periods of time together away from home especially the two Canadians, Phillip Anderson and Robert Peterson who were so far away from their homeland of Canada.

During my research, over the years, I have tried with little success to locate family members of the aircrew my dad flew with during his training and final posting to RAF 148 Special Duties Squadron stationed in Brindisi, Italy. In reading service reports of these men I know that they were together as crew from approximately end of September 1943 until their last flight together on August 4/5th 1944.

Four of crew had evaded capture and survived either in safe houses or marching with the partisans for so many months after they had baled out of Halifax JP 162FS-S. They returned to their homes in England and Canada.

No group crew photograph seems to exist of the McCall crew. I had no individual pictures of any of these men only those of my dad, but slowly one by one this changed. In looking through my family photos I came across a photo of my dad and another airman. On the back of the photo he had written "the other Upper Gunner and Me." This must be Clifford Aspinall. More recently in my searches for families of these airmen I began to gather further information. I heard, in March 2012, from Paul Frasier of Edinburgh, Scotland who is the grandson of Girvan McCall. He had found my name in one of the many postings I had made trying to find the crew and their families. He was able to provide me with photographs and general information of his grandfather.

I was later contacted by a Polish journalist Agnieszka Partridge who had been given a photograph by her grandmother of "two British pilots". This turned out to be Alan Jolly and Robert Peterson.

Now there were just two missing photos. During my visit to Krakow my friend Tomasz Jastrezsbki gave me a folder with letters, documents and photos and there in that folder were the photos of Charles Underwood and Phillip Anderson.

Now I could sit and look at the seven airmen who had become the aircrew of Halifax JP 162. What a wonderful feeling to see their faces.

I still felt the need to try and find family members connected to these men. Ever the optimist I wrote to local newspapers where two of the other airmen had lived and with an extraordinary piece of luck my request to the Blackpool Gazette was printed on October 15, 2013, the day I happened to be making a trip to England from my home in California. That same day I received an email from a Robert Jolly the son of Sgt Alan Jolly. We were able to meet and exchange information. A strange set of circumstances had brought us together and in the years I lived in England before coming to the USA, I had lived just a few miles from this family!

I had tried to contact Charles Underwood without success but I did meet with Agnieszka Partridge who had met with him several years ago and recorded his accounts. I have been unable to contact any family members for Clifford Aspinall. I had been told that his wife had never contacted any of the other crew members or their families after the loss of JP162. Of the two Canadians on this crew, I did receive information about Robert Orlando Peterson but nothing about Phillip James Anderson who had worked so tirelessly to bring these airmen safely home.

Flt. Lt. Girvan McCall RAFVR, Age 23
Service Number 127340
Post in Crew: Pilot
He served with148 Special Duties Squadron, Brindisi, Italy.
Date of Birth: 17 February, 1921.
Date of Marriage: 1943 to Catherine
Death August 5, 1944.

Girvan McCall as his family called him was the son of Peter
Charles Stewart McCall and Janet McCall. He had enlisted in the
Royal Air Force in Edinburgh as an airman in March 13, 1941.
He spent time in Canada training as a pilot. In September
1941 he was discharged and moved to the Arnold School in
the USA where I learned that he was training pilots. In 1942
James McCall began his second tour and was appointed to
a commission on August 5th 1942. In October 1943 he was
back in England at OTU (Operational Training Unit) at RAF
Finningly where he began further training and began the process
of "crewing up" becoming the "skipper" of the crew of Halifax
JP162 and part of 148 Squadron.

He was one of the crew who lost their lives after their airplane
Halifax JP 162 was shot down and crashed in the village of
Niecew. Flt. Lt. McCall was at first buried in Wojnarowa and
later re interred in Krakow Rakowicki Cemetery Grave1 E 11 by
CWWGC. Girvan McCall's wife Cathy is now 93 but in poor
health. They had a daughter Eileen.

Sgt Clifford Aspinall, RAFVR Age 37
Service Number: 2206350
Post in Crew: Upper Turret Gunner
He served with148 Special Duties Squadron, Brindisi, Italy.
Date of Birth: 8 July 1907
Date of Marriage: 1941
Date of Death: August 5th 1944.

Clifford Aspinall was from Blackpool, Lancashire and had enlisted in the RAF on 6th March 1943. He was promoted to Sergeant in October 1943, after completing his training as an Air Gunner. He was the oldest member of the McCall crew.

He was one of the three crew killed when the plane was shot down August 5 1944 in Niecew, Lesser Poland.

First buried in Wojnarowa then later moved to Rakowicki Cemetery Krakow Grave1 E 13. The first grave site in Wojnarowa has recently been found.

He was married, but I believe that they had not been married very long. His wife and family never contacted or gave any further information after he was killed.

I have no contact address or further information on Sgt Aspinall. I contacted the Blackpool Gazette newspaper in the hopes that I may get a response but sadly none came.

Sgt John Frederick Cairney Rae, RAFVR Age 33
Service Number: 2210115
Post in Crew: Rear Gunner
Enlisted: 25 May 1943
He was posted to 148 Squadron 22 May 1944
Date of Birth: 17 February 1911.
Date of Marriage: 18 April, 1938
Date of Death; 5 August 1944.
This is my Dad

He was born in Dalmuir, Scotland to Martin and Rose Ann Rae and had six brothers and one sister. His younger brother Frank served in the Merchant Navy during WW2.

John Rae served with 148 Special Duties Squadron, Brindisi Italy. This squadron was part of Balkan Air Force.

He was killed in the airplane when JP162 was attacked by a night fighter piloted by Konter. The plane crashed into a hillside in the village of Niecew. He and the other two crew killed were buried in the village of Wojnarowa. After the war these men were re-interred by Commonwealth War Graves Commission in Rakowicki Cemetery Krakow. Sgt Rae now rests in Grave 1 E 12. He and the other two airmen are buried next to each other.

The original grave/memorial site in Wojnarowa has been found recently.

My father was Fitters Mate in Civilian Life. He was married to Alice Johnson and had one daughter Rosemary Dawn Rae born 22/4/1944.

His wife Alice (known as Lal) died on November 6th, 1958.

As his daughter I am his closest living relative. He does have two granddaughters and four great grandsons as well as numerous great nephews and nieces. I have been researching his service for several years.

Sgt Walter Charles Underwood RAFVR, Age 20
Service Number: 1623931
Post in Crew: Engineer
He served with 148 Squadron Special Duties Squadron
Brindisi, Italy.
Date of Birth: March 22 1924
Date of Marriage: unknown
Date of Death: December 25 1997

He was a student before enlisting and came from Nasby, Yorkshire and was the youngest member of the crew. He was one four aircrew who baled out of the plane. He evaded capture and was rescued and served with the Home Army until he was able to return to England in approximately March 1945. He gave an evasion report to M I 9 on his return.

Latest information I have is from Agnieszka Partridge who is a Polish journalist and writer and works for Polish TV, Krakow. Several years ago she located Sgt. Charlie Underwood who was then living in Nottingham. Her grandparents were in the AK Army and her grandmother had given Agnieszka a photo of two "British Pilots" thought to be Sgt's Underwood and Peterson but in fact was Sgt's Jolly and Peterson from JP 162.

Charles Underwood was married to Beatrice and lived in Nottingham.

Sgt. Underwood died 1997.

Agnieszka recently tried to find Sgt Underwood and his family without success I have written to Nottingham newspapers hoping for a response but none came.

Sgt Alan Jolly, RAFVR, Age 22
Service Number: 1432300
Post in Crew: Wireless Operator/Air Gunner
He served with 148 Special Duties Squadron Brindisi, Italy.
Date of Birth: December 30 1921
Date of Death: July 12 1992

He baled out of plane evading capture. He was rescued by Home Army and served with them until he returned to the UK in March 1945. He was in a "safe house" in Tarnow and stayed there until the end of January 1945. Most of the time he was evading capture he was with Flt. Sgt. Robert Peterson, his fellow crewmate who was from Canada.

In my research I recently discovered he came from Fleetwood.

Further information has come to light that he did meet with Sgt. Walter Davis whose plane JP 244, piloted by P/O Tom Story, had engine problems and crashed in April 1944. All the crew survived but Sgt Davis had become separated and had been kept in a "safe house" for 5 months then handed over to the AK Army. He met up with the crew form my dad's plane when they were being transported home to the UK.

In recent attempts to find any family members of Sgt Alan Jolly, I wrote to a local paper in Fleetwood. The story was printed in the October 15, 2013 in the Blackpool Gazette edition and I was contacted by his son Robert on the same day. The timing was perfect as I had a trip planned to England and we were able to meet. This story continues.

F/O Phillip James Anderson, RCAF, Age 35
Service number: C11369
Post in Crew: Navigator
Enlisted in Toronto Canada: May 1 1942
Retired: September 6 1946
Date of Birth: 20 August 1909
Date of Marriage: unknown
Date of Death: unknown

He baled out of plane and was successful in evading capture. He served with the Home Army until he was able to return to England. Because of his rank he assumed the responsibility of trying and getting help for the evaders to get them home safely. He was mentioned in Dispatches with the award effective 13 June, 1946 as per London Gazette of that date and SFRO9. I believe this is from Royal Air Force Records dated 26 July 1946.

He evaded capture by the Germans and was helped by villagers near Tarnow He as well as the three other members of the JP 162 fought alongside the men in the AK Army.

He returned to England March 1945 and gave two evasion reports to MI. 9. One gave the details of his plane JP162 being shot down and another about his efforts to get the evading airmen home. In reading these reports, if the reader was not aware of the seriousness of the situation, some of his actions seemed almost comical but he did not give up his efforts in helping his fellow airmen from JP 162 but the many airmen who found themselves evading the German forces and who eventually made their way to Krakow in the hopes of finding transport home.

Phillip Anderson was an Economist in peacetime and came from Toronto, Canada. Sgt Charlie Underwood in a letter said F/O Anderson had returned to Canada after he left the RAFVR and he had had no further contact with him.

I have no contact with any family members.

Sgt. Robert Orlando Peterson, RCAF, Age 30
Service Number: R 131742
Post in Crew: Bomb Aimer
Enlisted: 21 September 1941.
He served with 148 Special Duties Squadron Brindisi, Italy.
Date of Birth: 19 April 1914.
Date of Marriage: unknown
Date of Death:

He was born in Banff, Alberta, and also resided in Revelstoke, British Columbia Canada where his step mother Mrs. A. Peterson lived. He was employed as a printer for the Banff "Crag Canyon" and before he enlisted worked at the Hanna Herald newspaper. I received this information on July 5th 2013 from the Revelstoke Museum. He was reported missing in August in the local paper Revelstoke Review. Later there was an article published in April 1945 saying he was safe in Odessa.

Sgt Peterson was one of the four aircrew of JP 162 who successfully baled out of the aircraft and evaded capture. He served in the Polish Home Army until his return via Odessa to the UK. He was given shelter in a "safe house" near Tarnow which was where the German High Commissioner was staying and the family who owned the home was also hiding a Jewish girl. On his return to England in March 1945 he gave

an evasion report to MI 9. According to Sgt. Charlie Underwood Sgt. Peterson returned to Canada.

In early May 2014 I was given information from a Frances Gates whose father had served with the 1586 Polish Flight based in Brindisi Italy with 148 Squadron. She had discovered a picture printed in the Macloud Gazette based in Fort Macloud of Robert Peterson taken at a presentation in Fort Macloud, Alberta, Canada where he was among a group of RCAF veterans being presented with the Bomber Command Clasp by the Canadian Minister of Veterans Affairs. Hopefully the story will continue.

CHAPTER 9

RAF 148 SPECIAL DUTIES SQUADRON

Motto "Trusty"
Badge
Two battle axes in saltire
The battle axes were selected as well tried
and formidable weapons
Authority
HM King George VI February 1938

148 Squadron[23] was originally formed on 10th February1918 in Andover as a night bombing unit. The squadron took the makeshift bombers it had to France in April 1918 and began by engaging in attacks on the enemy communications at the front and behind enemy lines and continued to operate in these outdated planes until the end of the war. It returned to England in 1919 and was disbanded at Tangmere on 30th June 1919.

The squadron was reformed on 7th June 1939 at Scampton as a light bomber squadron with Audaxes.[24] the squadron went through several changes because it was obvious that the aircraft it was operating were inadequate. The squadron added Wellesley[25] aircraft but these proved inadequate as a defensive aircraft for a European war. In March 1939 modern equipment such as the Wellingtons[26] were now being added. RAF 148 squadron then became the operational training unit for all the other units within the group and a move was made to Harwell at the outbreak of war. It was once again disbanded on April 9 1940 when it became No 15 Operational Training Unit (OTU).

When Italy entered the war in June, 1939 several detachments of UK Bomber squadrons were sent to Malta. Three of these from No 38, 99 and 115 squadrons were joined into the new 148 Squadron on December 14, 1940. The squadron continued attacks on Libya, Sicily and also the Italian mainland. They were still based in Malta until March 1941 and then they found a new home in Kabrit in Egypt. 148 Squadron supported the 8th Army and in December1942 a move of the squadron was made back to Malta where it was again disbanded and crews sent to join other units based on the island.

Loading supplies to drop to partisans. Photo courtesy of Larry Toft.

The Squadron reemerged in 14th March 1943 as the Special Liberator Flight (X Flight) at Gambut, Libya and thus was re designated as No 148 Squadron for special duties.

The squadron flew many different aircraft types. These included the Liberator[27] and Halifax planes which had been specially designed to be used in the dropping of arms and supplies to resistance groups in Albania, Greece and Yugoslavia. In January 1944 the squadron moved to a base in Southern Italy called Campo Casale, Brindisi. A Lysander[28] flight was added which was used for drop off and pick-up missions of agents and at the same time Halifax's replaced all the Liberators. Flights to Northern Italy Yugoslavia and Poland became the main operations that 148 Squadron undertook. The Halifax Bombers used by 148 Squadron were specially adapted for the purpose of dropping the supplies which the squadron was flying to the partisans in Yugoslavia and later to Poland.

Missions over the Balkans were the bulk of the work the squadron performed. They sent many missions to Poland in order to supply the partisan groups with much needed supplies often suffering heavy losses.

These flights were not protected by fighter escorts and losses were heavy due to heavy enemy fire and on some occasions from "friendly fire." These missions were classified as "secret" so our own forces were never sure when they saw unmarked planes pass in the dark.

All the flights that were flown by 148 Squadron were classed as secret so that in many cases it is still often difficult to obtain information about where they flew or the airmen who flew these highly classified missions.

At the end of the war the squadron was re-equipped with standard bomber Liberators and moved back to Egypt in November 1945 disbanding once again in January 1946.

By November 1946 it again became a functional squadron when it reformed once again this time at Upwood. It was now equipped with Lancaster's and Lincolns which were added in added in February 1950.

These aircraft took part in operations in Malaya during 1954 and 1955 but again the unit was disbanded in July 1955. 148 Squadrons last hurrah was when it formed again at Marham as a Valiant V-bomber unit in July 1956 because of the Suez crisis. Finally when it was discovered that there was metal fatigue in these aircraft the aircraft was grounded and 148 Squadron was finally disbanded in April 1965 after 47 years of service.

The airmen who flew with the Squadrons who had become part of the "Special Duties Squadrons" were never really recognized for the dangerous flights they flew night after night with little rest. Most of these flights have gone unrecorded. At some point in time no matter how good a crew you had become your "luck just ran out". The losses were staggeringly high!

CHAPTER 10

BALKAN AIR FORCE

**Air Vice Marshall William Elliot
and his successor George Mills.**

The Allied Military Policy in the Balkans was very simple "to provide the resistance movements with whatever direct air, military or naval support was required and to supply arms and equipment to aid their movement"

The Balkan Air Force as it became known was formed at the beginning of June 1944 and was made up of units from the Royal Air Force and the South African Air Force which were under the Mediterranean Allied Air Forces Command. This new group replaced the Desert Air Force which had at one time been responsible to supply the Special Duties Squadrons in the Balkans. There were various changes made on how the squadrons were to be assigned but the numbers of 18 Squadrons and 6 Supply Squadrons remained fairly constant. The group was now under the command of RAF Vice Marshals William Elliot and later his successor George Mills.

The surrender of Italy in September 1943 had not caused the Germans to leave the Balkans but instead they moved quickly to secure the Dalmatian coast and the islands which had been held by the Italians. The Balkan Air Force was the main supporter of the partisans in Yugoslavia led by Josip Broz Tito by dropping supplies, evacuating the wounded and dropping agents. This seemed a simple mission to carry out and it was largely due to these supplies that many of these resistance movements worked so efficiently but it was often at the high cost of Allied lives.

The Air Commander of the Group was responsible for overseeing of "Special Duties Squadrons." These squadrons were made up of fifteen different types of aircraft which were provided by eight different nationalities and the aircraft were flown to Italy, Czechoslovakia, Greece, Rumania, Bulgaria and Poland where they were able to deliver much needed supplies to the partisan groups of these countries. The Air Commander also worked closely with the Psychological Warfare Branch stationed in Bari, Italy organizing the dropping of leaflets called Nickels and other propaganda from as many missions as possible.

After becoming part of the Balkan Air Force in June 1944 RAF148 Squadron flew over 11,500 sorties which delivered 16,500 tons of much needed supplies, to which the partisans relied on. The squadron also flew 2,500 individuals into Yugoslavia. RAF148 Special Duties Squadron was able to fly 1500 sorties delivering approximately 2500 tons to Yugoslavia. These flights were much shorter in duration and often seemed almost a routine occurrence. The squadron made nearly 600 sorties to Greece. Twenty five flights were made to Bulgaria, 18 to Hungary, 37 to Czechoslovakia, and 31 to Austria, with few losses. The flights to Poland were less successful. Partisans were continually on the move, drop zones were often changed at the last moment and there was often poor communication. Aircraft and aircrew losses on these flights were high. During the Uprising in August 1944, 217 sorties were attempted with only 104 being successful with huge losses of aircraft and aircrews.

The Polish partisan forces finally surrendered in Warsaw and when that event took place the war effort of RAF148 Squadron and the Polish 1586 squadron, of flying the necessary supplies, declined to about 15 flights a month. The squadron carried out a brief period of general transport duties in Italy before moving to Egypt where it was disbanded on 15th January, 1946. As late as 1956 the squadron had again reformed and was sent to aid in the Suez Operations. In 1965 148 Squadron was finally disbanded after a long and distinguished service with the help of some of the finest airmen. These included seven very special airmen and their plane Halifax JP 162FS-S.

CHAPTER 11

FINALLY TO BRINDISI

Finally word came of the McCall aircrew posting, to RAF 148 Special Duties Squadron at Campo Casale, Brindisi, Italy.

Aircrews who became part of special duties squadron were some of the finest. They were selected only after extensive rigorous tests for their physical character and intelligent flying aptitude. Very little is known about these airmen mainly because of the types of missions they were flying, and perhaps because of this it often seems they have been forgotten. Many of these airmen when they did return to civilian life spoke little of their experience.

The McCall crew had finally been posted to an operational squadron far from home

John Rae left home this time to join his crew and his new Squadron. His posting in late May 1944 would take him first to North Africa which was part of the Central Mediterranean Force and then in early June to RAF 148 Special Duties Squadron in Brindisi , Italy. The squadron had become part of the Balkan Air Force which had the responsibility to supply the Yugoslavia partisans and later to fly much needed supplies to northern Italy and Poland.

The Allied invasion of the mainland of Italy which began on September 3 1943 eventually led to Italy being secured and the new opportunity of having bases set up and built for the RAF on the airfields abandoned by the Germans in Southern Italy. This, it was thought, would help make the flights to Poland a little shorter. Flights still were over twelve hours in length flying over 1600 miles round trip much over enemy territory with treacherous flying over the Carpathian Mountains and the heavily defended Luftwaffe base at Krakow. The aircrews also flew missions to Northern Italy and Yugoslavia dropping supplies and agents. Missions to Yugoslavia, it seemed, were the shortest and easiest.

The Special Operations missions of 148 Squadron were so secret that the airmen themselves often did not know of their operation destination and certainly families did were no aware what these airmen were doing. Their letters home were censored. In my dad's censored letter home to his sister Margaret on May 29, 1944 he was his usual caring self, making sure everyone was being taken care of including my mother who he thought "might be feeling pretty low" so he told his sister "write to her often." He ends saying "well I can't tell you much about this place but I think North Africa is OK".

I believe at that time he was with his crew at No 2 Aircrew Reception center which was RAF Rabat Sale in North Africa. Records show that they had flown from England on the 22nd May and successfully delivered their aircraft. They then moved to No1 Base Personnel Depot to await their final posting to 148 Squadron. Due to the hand writing on John Rae's records it looks as though he joined the unit on 22 June but this is clearly incorrect as the McCall crew began their operational flights in early June. Their actual date of arrival is not recorded on the ORB (Operation Record Book) at that time. The McCall crew finally arrived in Brindisi, Italy probably wondering what lay ahead.

The living conditions of 148 Squadron at Campo Casale,[29] where not exactly like staying at "the Ritz". They were certainly

**1944 Brindisi tented camp taken by Roger Alves
of 148 Squadron Ground crew. Photo courtesy
of his son Steve Alves**

far more basic then they had been used to during their training
in England or those of their fellow Bomber Command crews
who were still based in England.

The priorities of the "powers that be" were to have a workable
airbase with usable runways and planes ready to fly on the long
missions. It seems the comfort of the airmen came second. The
aircrew's who were unfortunate enough to be the first based at
Brindisi were largely left to fend for themselves as the huts
being constructed for their living quarters were nowhere near to
completion. Their "home away from home" was a tent with no
beds! There were four men to a tent. Many of the airmen
showed their inventive skills by constructing their beds from
what they could find. Sanitary facilities were basic. One bath a
week, soap rationed to one small bar, blankets put outside daily
to air and men told to keep the areas in their tents clean sometimes an impossible task with the winds continually blowing the
sand everywhere. There were long walks to the Mess.

It was hard to keep things dry when there was wet weather.
Crews often flew in damp flying clothes and crews often

wondered that if their parachutes were damp would they have opened. I hope that worry was never put to the test.

There was also a problem of tires on the aircraft splitting as the planes took off and landed on the rough runways at Brindisi. This of course could prove disastrous to the aircrews. There were rumors amongst the airmen of No 334 wing that there was a supply of tires at Bari. Plans were set in motion to "acquire a few of these spare tires" and the men managed to remove fourteen from the supply and have them fitted to their own planes. The owners of the tires from No 204 group were not amused and demanded that No 334 wing return the tires. The only response that they received from No 334 wing and No 148 squadron was "the show must go on!"

Food supplies were as much a problem as hygiene. Rationing of food supplies was a source of discontent especially with the medical officer who when he had spoken with the crews decided that he needed to make an official report. He wondered "how it was possible to expect these airmen to continue flying long missions with such basic supplies as:

I small packet of biscuits

A packet of glucose sweets

One small slab of chocolate which was often frozen

One small pack of chewing gum.

The conditions these airmen were expected to live[30] and still fly these dangerous missions night after night makes me wonder how they managed to live their daily lives in very basic and often poor conditions.

At the time of James McCall's crew's arrival in early summer maybe the conditions at the base were not quite so bad but

I have been told that during the long cold winter months conditions were harsh. Horror stories have been heard and told about the custom of raiding the tents of those crews who did not return, taking the little luxuries that they no longer needed. Crews who did not return were not talked about by their fellow airmen. I have often wondered what happened to the possessions of my dad's crew when they failed to return on their last mission on August 4/5th 1944. Hopefully their possessions were sent home to their families.

And so they arrived. Sad to say crews were never formally welcomed or introduced to the squadron so when they attended their first "Ops Briefing" it was as if they had been part of the squadron and knew all the "rules and regulations". The McCall crew settled in as best they could, seven airmen, far from home but a team who relied on each other in the air and I am sure supported each other on the ground. They met the other crews at the briefing room, but often were assigned to different missions, taking off and landing at different times. No information about the losses in the squadron was given to the crews or news of a crew or crews who did not return. Most crews were never told the odds but I am sure that most knew. Often aircrew carried a small amulet such as a coin or a rabbit's foot.

Each member of an aircrew in the Special Operations Units attended the briefing for the missions that they would carry out. They were given the location of the drop zones as well as the enemy's front line. It was felt that each crew member share all this information so that it would help them to work better as a complete team. The pilots could plan the safest routes and the navigator added his own codes and maps information so that they could together plan the best route for that particular missions drop zones. These flights were difficult from a navigator's point of view because they flew solely by pinpointing. All aircrew had been trained for the possibility of having to "bale out of the aircraft" and given orders to avoid capture. The crew received those instructions during a two week Evasion Course in England before joining their squadron. Maybe it was because of lessons learned on that course that Sgt's Jolly, Peterson, Underwood and F/O Anderson were able to evade capture on the fateful night of August 4/5 1944.

RAF 148 Squadron shared this base with other squadron's 1586 Polish Special Duties Flight and 31 Squadron of the South African Air Force. I wonder if the McCall crew ever met up with any of the men from the Polish squadron who they had trained with in 18 OTU (Operational Training Unit) in England so many months ago.

Operations were stressful and perilous and there was a high chance of being attacked and having to bale out or worse being killed. It was physically demanding and having to be constantly alert for many hours at a time often having to endure noisy, cramped and cold conditions, the smell of fuel on a plane often packed with explosives caused a lot of stress. These crews flew in total darkness, alone and with no fighter protection and no communications to avoid being seen or heard by the enemy.

Fatigue and fear and general combat stress after going on operations "night after night" meant some of the aircrew succumbed to these harsh conditions and had "Lack of moral fiber" written on their records and were removed from duty so that they would not affect the moral of the airmen they flew with. In one example a crew was known to refuse to fly with their pilot even though they themselves could possibly face disciplinary action. In many ways in my opinion this was a harsh term to write on anyone's record but who am I to criticize.

Survival was the overriding instinct each airman had and by working together as a team relying on each others skills during these long flights so they were glad to complete each mission and return safely to base hopefully for a warm meal and warm bed.

As I think about the long flights that these airmen flew often 10 to 12 hours long I can compare them with my flight from California to England or Europe which are roughly the same length but in comparative comfort! I can relate to how draining on the system that is. How these men flew these flights night after night under very different circumstances I will never know!

The squadron had been successful in dropping supplies and slowly they were able to achieve a record number of successful drops to the partisans. They received encouragement from Air Marshall Slessor and received his congratulations.

Conditions may have been harsh but these airmen were resilient, organizing "Gala Days" which included serious competition as wall as fun events such as boat races in boats the men had built. Cups and medals were presented at the end of the day. The airmen seemed to have teams for everything from football matches which culminated in a Cup Final. All of these events were well supported both on and off the field. In summer there were cricket matches to enjoy. It seemed as though these airmen were just trying to bring all the normal activates to Brindisi that they would have enjoyed if they had been at home. These events were in fact planned to keep spirits of the aircrews high. It gave the aircrew something else to talk about and of course there was great rivalry amongst the men as to who were the best teams. There always seems to be someone who is good at organizing and enthusiastic about making the most out of a bad situation.

My dad, always the joker, would in his letters home even though they were censored, tease his sister Margaret about "the ice cream cone he was enjoying," obviously fully aware of the strict rationing in place in Britain. He had apparently always been full of fun and it seems he still had his keen sense of humor even in these trying circumstances.

Despite all the difficulties and challenges the McCall crew and all the other crews attached to this base knew they were there to carry out missions to aid countries like Yugoslavia, North Italy and Poland by dropping supplies and agents. This they did night after night without realizing how brave they were. The flights they made were long and exhausting. The crews showed the highest degree of courage and determination. They were simply "doing their bit" and that "bit' meant flying these missions night after night.

After settling in to their new surroundings it wasn't long before the McCall crew began their first operational flights.

The aircrew of Halifax JP 162F-S for sugar flew their first missions to Northern Italy and Yugoslavia and later to Poland dropping supplies and agents. Missions to Yugoslavia were the shortest and easiest. Flights to Poland were another matter. The nearly 1600 mile return flight over Yugoslavia, Hungry and the Carpathian mountains with only a short period of summer darkness was a hazardous one. Supplies had to be dropped from below 400ft. with speed reduced to 150 mph in the hope that they would fall in the relatively small areas held by the Poles.

In letters I received from my friend Piotr Hodra from "Operations Dark of the Moon" he shared with me information about my dad John Rae and about the flights my dad and his crew made. I had been finding it very difficult in gathering this information but he was able to obtain it from Polish documents. I have since obtained the Operation Records for 148 Squadron.

At the time the McCall crew joined 148 Special Duties Squadron it was flying operations to support various partisan units including Force 399 a Special Operations Executive (SOE) unit which had been set up to work with the partisan units in Yugoslavia, Albania and Hungary, No 1 unit which aided partisans in Northern Italy and the American Office of Strategic Services (OSS) and the Inter-Service Liaison Department which was a cover name for the British Secret Intelligence Service (MI6)

All these operations which the squadron carried out were given numerous code names. The operations the McCall crew carried out and the organizations that they were conducted on behalf included.[31]

FORCE 399	FORCE 1	FORCE OSS	ISLD (MI6)	OTHERS
Brasenose	Baltimore	Charleston	Sirene	Bamberg
Cockold	Beach	Stutz		Evaston
Conserve	Lamberton			Polish
Decima	Loxton			A138
Geisha	Lutley			201
Gilgal				Seaport
Icarus				

McCALL CREW OPERATIONS:

After settling in to their new "digs" the McCall crew was finally ready to begin their operational flying. When the "ops" list was posted and the crews who were "down for flying" went out to the aircraft they had been assigned and began checking everything. In the case of my dad he would check the guns, gyro sight in the turret for elevation and its rotation including the Dead mans handle. This was the safety lock system on the guns which prevented them firing by accident. When the gunner released hold of the guns they would not fire. He would make sure the turret was absolutely clean and the gun armourer's had not left anything that would jam the ammo belts or the turrets movement. The Perspex covering had to be clean and have no scratches which could distract him when they were flying in darkness. He would check his oxygen supply and anything else he thought needed to be taken care of before the long flight. The crew would then go and check their flying gear and perhaps write letters home to their loved ones, enjoy a meal and then wait for the final "ops" briefing.

While the airmen checked each of their stations on the plane the ground crew would be loading the canisters and packages which would be dropped at the mission drop zone as well as fuelling the plane.

Andrew Bennett a relative of Flt. Sgt. Alex Bennett RAAF (Royal Australian Air Force) 148 Squadron who flew with the Crabtree crew in JP181 on one of their mission gave a nice scenario of his uncle, Alex Bennett, and my dad John sitting sharing a meal together before their final briefing and flight. As the McCall crew walked into the briefing room on that first night they saw a large map of the Balkans and finally saw where they were headed that night. There would probably a moment of silence with everyone sucking in their breath and then of

Operations Briefing. Courtesy of Operation Dark of the Moon website

course someone would maybe break the silence with some witty comment! These meetings were held to give all the aircrews involved information of their destinations and actions to be taken. On each mission they flew there was a special code name given and any instructions that the officers in charge deemed necessary. Each aircrew would sit together and listen to all the instructions and would set about taking care of last minute preparations. Each of the crews usually had different take of times and would often be flying to different drop zones.

The McCall crew like the other crews would then head off to collect their flying kit, flying rations, escape kit and parachutes. Then off to the crew truck and out to the dispersal point. They would climb aboard and settle in doing all their pre check routine and then it was time to take off and fly to their destination. Depending on this their flight time could be up to ten hours or longer and on return their day wasn't over until they had been de-briefed, written reports, checked any damage to their aircraft, after which the crew had a meal and then to bed. Waking up a few hours later they would check the "ops" list to see if they were "down for flying" or maybe on a rare occasion have a night off.

I wonder what they all thought as this new phase in their working together as a crew began. This McCall flew a total of 28 sorties before their final flight! [32]

JUNE 1944 MISSIONS:

June 9/10 1944 On the McCall crew's first operational mission they undertook when they finally arrived at Brindisi they flew in JP286 (S) on Operation "ICARUS 5" which was to Mikylus in Yugoslavia. They were able to drop 15 containers and 27 packages before they flew on to Prijedor the second drop area where the dropped 300 lbs of nickels (leaflets). When they finally returned to base and were landing the aircraft had a burst tire. No one was hurt but it was an interesting start to their operational flying!

The Nickels (leaflets) the aircrews dropped were in fact propaganda. Often when these were dropped from about 12,000 feet it could take sometimes an hour for them to finally flutter to the

Loading nickels pamphlets.
Operation Dark of
the Moon website.

ground. This in fact meant that these leaflets were often scattered over a wide area making them more difficult for the enemy to collect.

Most of the supplies which were dropped consisted of arms and ammunition which included the ammunition for the types of guns used by the partisans. In the winter months supplies would probably include warm clothing, boots, food and medical supplies.

The crew flew their next three operations in BB338 which was code named "ICARUS 7."

Loading supplies at Brindisi.
Photo courtesy of Larry Toft.

June 10/11 This time they were able to drop another 15 containers and 26 packages and 300 lbs of nickels were dropped at a place called Obrovac in Yugoslavia.

June 13/14 On this flight the code name was "ICARUS 10 and "Operation A138".

This mission was unsuccessful because of ground haze at the drop zone.

June 14/15 The third operation in BB338 was "COCKOLD 10" near Ljubljana followed but on their return the crew had to divert to GROTTAGUE because of strong cross winds at Brindisi. They were flown back to base by Squadron Leader Dunphy and arrived back at their home base on June 19, 1944.

I am sure there was celebration when the McCall crew heard that Flying Officer Phillip Anderson, RCAF, the navigator from their crew, was appointed Officer in Charge of Air Sea Rescue.

The McCall crew was then sent to Maison Blanche in Northern Africa which was the location of No.144 Maintenance Unit to collect one of the two returning aircraft for the squadron. These were KB154 or KB147 which had been flown to this large maintenance depot for maintenance. They arrived back in Brindisi in time to take part in their next mission.

June 23/24 flying in DG357 (O) "GILGAL B4 to Kolasin in Montenegro and were able to deliver 15 containers and 54 packages and then they flew on to Ubli and Kloport where they made a success drop of 500 lbs of nickels (leaflets).

June 26/27 Two nights later flying in JN 897 (T) the McCall crew flew operation "EVASTON" but abandoned the flight because of heavy cloud and icing on the way to their target.

The next three nights the McCall crew found themselves in the same aircraft flying three successful trips to "BRASENOSE 10"

June 28/29 (15 containers and 26 packages) to Konec then to "DECIMA 9" 29/30 June (15containers and 36 packages) and their final trip on June 30/July1 to "CONSERVE 10" here they dropped (15 containers and 28 packages).

All the flights flown by McCall Crew in June were to Yugoslavia or Italy. On several occasions their flights were diverted to other airfields because of severe crosswinds, or aircraft problems and they were either flown back to their base in Brindisi or more often transported back by road.

JULY 1944 MISSIONS:

For the next two flights in July my dad John Rae is not included in the McCall flight crew roster which on

July 2/3 were code named "GEISHA 102"

July 3/4 code name "SAVANNA 102"

On July 3 148 Squadron suffered four losses. Once again the squadron lost valuable crews. On the day following these tragic losses my dad's pilot James McCall was promoted to Acting Flt. Lt. A somewhat subdued celebration took place.

July 4/5 The McCall crew on this mission flew in a Halifax V DG357. The code name was "CONSERVE 10" and this saw them on another return flight to Stajovce to deliver 15 Containers and 65 packages. Like several of their previous flights they had a second drop zone on the same mission on this occasion dropping 300 lbs. of nickels. My dad rejoins the crew on this flight.

July 6/7 The "CHARLSTON 12" mission on behalf of the OSS to Borg oval di Tara in Northern Italy was flown in Halifax V DG357 (O). They had flown this aircraft on their June 23/24 missions. On this mission the McCall crew was able to drop 15 Containers and 14 packages with 300 lbs. of nickels being delivered to Chiavari.

July 7/8 this according to the Squadron record Books was their first flight on a Polish mission known by code name OPERATION 201. Most of the flights to Poland simply had numbers for their code names. The mission had to be abandoned when the arrived at the drop zone and no reception party was located in the target area. This occurred quite often on the Polish missions as the partisans were continually on the move. The McCall crew returned to base.

July 9/10 On this mission called "ICARUS 111" they attempted to carryout their mission but there was heavy cloud and zero visibility which forced the crew to abandon another mission. However on the return journey to base their aircraft DG357 developed a hydraulic failure and Flt Lt. McCall was forced to carry out a belly landing on arrival at Brindisi. All of the crew escaped uninjured but the aircraft was out of commission. On this flight they had an extra airman F/O J. Wilson who was probably training.

For the next two days the McCall crew was not on the roster to fly and no operations were possible on July 12 or 13 because of poor weather conditions. Probably for the McCall crew this was a welcome respite and they were able to get some much needed rest.

July 14. My father John Rae was part of the crew Flt. Lt. McCall took with him to No 144 MU to ferry a new aircraft back to the squadron. This was the arrival of JP162 which was given the code 'S' This plane was to replace one of the planes lost on the night of July 3/4th. On arrival back to Brindisi the next night McCall and is crew flew their first mission on "their plane."

July 16/17 The McCall crew took "S" on the "BEACH 4" mission to support Force 1 but there were no reception parties waiting at either primary or secondary targets so the task was abandoned. However on their return flight the aircraft was beginning to run short of fuel so the 15 containers and 3 packages were jettisoned near the primary target after a signal of three fires was seen nearby. They also dropped 200 lbs. of nickels near Chiavari.

July 17/18 on JP254 D they flew to another destination code name "LOXTON 10" and they were able to drop 15 containers and 15 packages to Italian partisans on behalf of Force 1 and flowed up by dropping 200 lbs. of nickels at Massa.

July 19/20 Flying in BB196 a mark V Halifax coded E on another OSS operation called "STUTZ" and they were able to deliver successfully 14 containers and 23 packages to Monte Cavallo but because of heavy cloud it was decided by McCall not to drop the "Special Container." There is no record of what was in this container.

July 21/22 they flew once again in JP254 D on mission "LAMBERTON 107"for Force 1 and Sirene for ISLD where they made another successful delivery of 12 containers and 13 packages at 44:22N 10:27E Lamberton target but the Sirene target was hidden by heavy cloud so 200 lbs of nickels were dropped over Brescia.

July 22 The McCall crew did not fly.

The crew flew three more "LAMBERTON" sorties. These missions were all to Northern Italy.

July 23/24 "LAMBERTON 109" flown in JP181 X. On this mission they were successful in dropping15 containers and 18 packages and 200lbs of nickels over Massa but on their there return flight to Brindisi they had to divert and land at Celone because of ground haze.

Dropping supplies for the partisans. Photo courtesy of John Heaton.

July 24/25 "LAMBERTON 112" flown in JP295 P they dropped 15 containers and 15 packages plus 200lbs of nickels at La Spezia.

July 25/26 this time the McCall crew operated JP162 S which was the aircraft they had ferried back form No 144 Maison Blanche on July 19 1944... On this mission they had a successful drop of 15 containers and 16 packages and a further 200 lbs. of nickels at their destination which was again at La Spezia. They had to divert to Grottaglia owing to a severe cross wind at Brindisi and this resulted in them not taking part in the following night's operations on July 26/27 but they were back at Brindisi and ready to be part of the next mission.

July 27/28 Flying in JP162 S this mission had a code names of "LUTLEY106" 44:23N 10:33E. They were able to deliver 15 containers and 20 packages before they dropped 200lbs nickels at Viareggio.

July 28/29 The McCall crew returned to the "LAMBERTON" mission no.125 again in JP162 S with 14 containers and 22 packages being diverted. They followed this off by releasing 200lbs nickels over Viareggio.

July 30/31 For this flight the McCall crew were briefed that they had two target areas for this mission. Code name was "LOXTON" drop area 42:23N 10:33E and secondary drop area was Bamberg. The actual location for the second drop is not identified in the operation record book. They were able to drop 15 containers and 6 packages successfully at LOXTON drop zone but there was no reception party at Bamberg so they diverted and dropped another 200 lbs. of nickels at Viareggio.

There were no operations scheduled for the night of July 31 and the McCall crews were not rostered for operations on August 1. This was another rare chance for them to rest for a couple of days.

AUGUST 1944 MISSIONS:

August 2/3 The McCall crew were back flying JP 162 S with another duel operation code names "SEAPORT" (Asti) and "BALTAMORE " (Ceva) with 15 containers being dropped at Asti and 4 personnel and 7 packages at Ceva plus 200lbs. nickels being dropped over Allassio on the return journey to Brindisi. On this mission the McCall crew was joined by Flt. Sgt Atkin.

All the flights the McCall crew had flown so far on their arrival to 148 Special Duties Squadron stationed at Brindisi had been to Yugoslavia and to Northern Italy. These had been shorter and somewhat safer missions than one what was to occur the following evening.

August 4/5 Flying once again they flew in JP 162 FS S for sugar to a destination in Poland. The Warsaw Uprising had begun on August 1st and the partisans were in desperate need of supplies. The crew was given a special mission to help the Polish Home Army. Their destination changed at the last minute to a safer drop zone rather than flying to Warsaw which was now in the midst of the Warsaw Uprising and was heavily defended. Simply put in the Operations record book "JP 162 took off and nothing further was heard for this aircraft. FTR" (Failed to Return).

Contrary to common belief or perception aircrews did not have their "own" aircraft. They did not always fly the same plane. Aircraft were often scheduled for routine maintenance or in need of repair so the aircrew flew their missions in the available aircraft. Throughout their missions together the majority of the flights the McCall crew flew were on Halifax JP 162F-S

It is sad that even long after hostilities ended these airmen were all but forgotten. We will never know if this was because the missions they flew were too secret to be talked about. It is only now seventy years later that people like me, the families and loved ones of those aircrews are learning the full story of 148 Special Duties Squadron. We may never know the reason.

CHAPTER 12

THE WARSAW UPRISING BEGINS

On August 1st 1944 while my father and the McCall crew were stationed at Brindisi the Warsaw Uprising began. General Bor- Komorosky gave the order for the AK (Home Army) in Polish known as Armia Karjowra to "rise against the enemy." Partisans flooded out of the sewers in Warsaw, surprising the German army, and began the brutal fight to regain their beloved city of Warsaw. Within five days they had seventy percent of the city in their control. The Uprising would last sixty-three days with a tremendous loss of life and the destruction of Warsaw. Records show that over 200,000 people perished during the uprising. By 1945 the population of the city was only about 1000 men living in the ruined buildings. The Polish Government in London asked the Russians for help, it was refused and so while the city was being fought for so heroically by the partisans, the Russian Army, who were part of the Allied Forces, sat on the other side of the Vistula River and did nothing.

Allied Support for Warsaw

Selected Documents sent on the fourth and fifteenth days of the Warsaw Uprising record the following messages:

Aug. 4, 1944 message from Winston Churchill to Josef Stalin:[33]

> "At urgent request of Polish Underground Army we are drop-ping, subject to weather, about sixty tons of equipment and ammunition into the southwest quarter of Warsaw, where it is

said a Polish revolt against the Germans is in fierce struggle. They also say that they appeal for Russian aid, which seems to be very near. They are being attacked by one and a half German divisions. This may be of help in your operation."

Aug. 15, 1944 Andre Y. Vyskinsky, First Assistant to the People's Commissar for Foreign Affairs of the Soviet Union, message to Ambassador Harrison in Moscow: [34]

"The Soviet Government cannot of course object to English or American aircraft dropping arms in the region of Warsaw, since this is an American and British affair. But they decidedly object to American or British aircraft, after dropping arms in the region of Warsaw, landing on Soviet territory, since the Soviet Government does not wish to associate themselves either directly or indirectly with the adventure in Warsaw."

The Polish people were in desperate need of supplies. The British Government had decided that as the Russian army was not going to cross the Vistula River to aid the partisans that they must continue to drop supplies even though the Russians had refused Allied Aircraft to land on Russian soil even if the planes might be badly damaged. Flights from Britain, a journey of 2000 miles, were out of the question so Churchill ordered that relief be flown from Italy. This was against his better judgment.

The Uprising news had not reached 148 Special Duties Squadron or 1586 Polish Flight in Brindisi, Italy. Sorties that had been planned on August 1st were cancelled because of bad weather. RAF 148 Squadron had planned seven sorties to Poland. Two flights were cancelled, one returned early and three were successful.

On the fourth day of the Uprising August 4th 1944, the airmen in Brindisi from RAF 148 Squadron and the Polish 1568 squadron were briefed on what was happening and were told in no uncertain terms "they were on no account to fly to Warsaw. It was far too dangerous". Seven crews from each squadron heard this message at the Operations Meeting. They were given different "safer drop zones".

The 1600-mile round trip flight from Brindisi, Italy over Yugoslavia, Hungary and the Carpathians, with only a short period of summer darkness was a hazardous one. Supplies had to be dropped from below 400ft with airspeed reduced to 150 mph in the hope that they would fall in the relatively small areas held by the Poles. Drop zone areas were marked by the partisans with torches.

And so it was that on August 4th shortly before 20:00 fourteen four engine bombers took off from the airbase at Campo Casale, Brindisi, Italy. The squadron flights flew these missions without fighter escort. Each plane usually flew alone to its destination as crews became aware that flying several of these heavy bombers flying together made them even more vulnerable. That night seven of the airplanes were from 1586 Flight Special Duties Squadron of the Polish Air Force and seven were from RAF 148 Special Duties Squadron. The planes were heavily loaded, and in fact exceeded the permitted take –off weight, with supplies for the Polish AK Army who were fighting to win back their beloved Warsaw. These aircrews had had their orders changed by Marshall John Slessor. Warsaw was heavily defended by the Germans using anti aircraft guns. Despite the warning not to fly to Warsaw four of the Polish crews disobeyed.

Things started badly for 148 Squadron when one of the planes piloted by Sgt. Snow LW284Z which had been borrowed from the Polish Squadron had to return because the guns in the rear turret would not fire. A tire on the plane burst on landing and the undercarriage collapsed and the plane burst into flames. It was totally destroyed but the crew was safe. This blocked the runway at Brindisi for quite some time. For the RAF crews who obeyed and flew to the "safe drop zones" on August 4/5th 1944 they were not quite so lucky. This turned out to be one of the most tragic missions for the squadron and for those brave crews. W/O French in another aircraft Halifax IN897T had no option but to dump its cargo after the port engine had failed, and the aircraft of W/O Brown in Halifax JP295 returned after they received no reception from the drop zone area. The plane had to land at Grottaglie because the runway at Brindisi was still blocked by the earlier crash. Even worse news was yet to come. The other four aircraft FTR, these were the aircraft piloted by F/L King in EB147K, all of the aircrew survived the crash but became POW's, Flt. /Lt. Arnold Blynn in JP276A and his crew had volunteered to fly on this mission. All the crew members were killed. P/O Crabtree in JP181X (all crew were killed) and lastly F/L McCall in JP162FS, (three crew were killed and four baled out and evaded capture). This was my father's plane in which he was the rear gunner Seventeen airmen from 148 Squadron lost their lives, seven became POW and four managed to evade capture. The Polish Squadron lost one plane, but even though it was damaged it did manage to return to base where it crashed.

Aug.4/5 1944 Map of Crash sites.

Crash Sites of RAF Supply Aircraft on August 4/5th1944 MissionEB147K King Crew, JP276A Blynn Crew, JP181X Crabtree Crew, JP162FS McCall Crew[36]

In early September 1944 the Russians finally agreed to cooperate but by then the Polish, RAF and SAAF units had lost 31 aircraft out of 181 which had been dispatched in the 22 nights of operations.

With this terrible loss to the squadron Marshall John Slessor[34] told the powers that be:

"I am not unconscious of the fact that Commanders must accept casualties for what are narrowly called political reasons and it is because of that reason alone which precluded me from refusing absolutely to send anymore aircraft to Warsaw."

By making that statement Slessor did not intend to send any further missions to Poland in that phase of the moon. The usual politicking began but for two days Slessor stood firm. On the seventh of August he gave in and flights to Poland resumed. This he said was against "my conscience and with great reluctance." The Polish crews were anxious to fly to help their fellow countrymen. The crews from 1586 Polish Squadron flew but Marshall John Slessor continued to refuse to allow the RAF crews to fly until the last quarter of the moon.

CHAPTER 13

THE LAST FLIGHT OF JP162FS

Halifax

Halifax JP 162FS-S for sugar of 148 Special Duties Squadron was one of the seven RAF planes that had left Campo Casale on the long and dangerous flight to Poland on the night of August 4 1944.

Aircrew was:

Flight Lt. James McCall RAFVR pilot, F/O P.J. Anderson RCAF Navigator, Sgt. R.O. Peterson RCAF Air/Bmr, Sgt. W.C Underwood RAFVR Flt /Eng, Sgt. A. Jolly RAFVR RAFVR W/Op, Sgt. C. Aspinall RAFVR Air/Gnr. and my dad Sgt John F.C. Rae RAFVR Air/Gnr.

They took off from their base at Campo Casale, Brindisi on August 4th at about 19:00 hours on a special mission code name "Operation Polish 211" their destination was Miechow about 30 KM north of Krakow a long night flight over occupied and heavily defended Europe. The drop off area was marked by the partisans with torches so Halifax JP 162 FS-S was able to make a successful drop at the drop zone "KARAREK" and John Rae the rear gunner and Robert Peterson the bomb aimer reported to their skipper that their drop was successful at the designated drop zone. The pilot Flt. Lt. James McCall then turned the plane around and headed on the long journey home to Brindisi.

The aircrew worked well together and the pilot James McCall and his two gunners Clifford Underwood and John Rae had become a very closely knit team particularly with the possibility they could be attacked by night fighters. The rear gunner, my father was also the protector of the men flying on JP162.

The gunners were the eyes of the pilot always searching the sky and with their help the pilot was usually able instead of flying straight to turn up or down at the last second and spoil the aim of the fighter. This gave his gunners the advantage of using their heavy machine guns. On this mission, however, that strategy did not work.

On the return journey at about 01:30am JP 162 was attacked by a Ju.88 a twin engine plane flown by the Luftwaffe who had a base in Krakow. They were often called night fighters. It was flown by Feldwebel Helmut Konter from 3/NJG 100 base in Krakow who approached the Halifax from the rear and underneath. The fighter opened fire hitting my dad John Rae and setting alight the auxiliary fuel tanks of the Halifax. Flt. Lt. McCall stayed with the aircraft but he, rear gunner Sgt. Rae, and the mid upper gunner Sgt. Aspinall who were unable to bale out of the plane and were killed.

The "skipper" James McCall had given the order to "abandon aircraft" and four of the crew Anderson, Peterson. Underwood and Jolly were able to do so by parachuting from the burning aircraft at about 7000 feet. On that disastrous night because of the quick thinking of their skipper these four airmen on JP 162 were able to parachute to the ground from their burning aircraft. They did not know what was facing them and the fact that they would need all the skills they possessed to live in hiding and on the run for seven months.

Halifax JP 162FS-S crashed into a small hillside in the village of Niecew some 80km SE of Krakow. People of the local villages were able to hastily bury these men, I am told, under the orders of the Germans who had a garrison in the area, in the village of Wojnarowa. They were later re-interred by the Commonwealth War Graves Commission in the Commonwealth Section of Rakowicki Cemetery, Krakow.

Sgt Underwood was the first to leave the plane by the front exit followed by Anderson the navigator, Peterson the bomb aimer and the lastly Jolly the wireless operator. It was a clear night and the first thought of the airmen as they floated to the ground, was to get their bearings and hope that they had not been spotted by German troops. As they floated down they recalled how peaceful and quiet it was after the roar of the engines. Sergeant Underwood said that he could see the burning plane in the distance. He and Sgt. Jolly landed approximately 17 km north of Nowy Sacz, about half a mile from where the aircraft crashed in the village of Niecew. Sgt. Charlie Underwood describes burying his parachute and hearing someone coming down the lane whistling. It was Sgt. Alan Jolly. Charlie Underwood later recalled that when he realized that it was Alan Jolly whistling he said it reminded him more of an English country lane and not the enemy territory where he actually was. They made their way to the burning plane to see if anyone was trapped. When they finally reached the wreckage they realized there was nothing they could do to help their skipper and the two gunners. No one had survived so they had to reluctantly walk away.

They knew it was important to get away from the area where the plane had crashed as quickly as possible as they were sure that German troops in the area would make their way to the wreckage. Shortly after they met up with some Poles and Charlie Underwood told them who they were and they were taken to a nearby house and given food and drink and hidden.

On August 6th they were given the choice of being handed over to the Germans or joining the partisans. They joined the partisans! They were told that they would have to go on a long march. This group of partisans belonged to Battalion III "Gorlice" under the command of "Michala." For the next five or six weeks Underwood and Jolly marched and worked with the partisans doing sabotage work. When their footwear gave out they asked to hideout for a while. The Germans at that time were again rounding up young men for forced labor so Underwood age 20 and Jolly age 22 were taken to a "safe house" near Jaslow where they stayed with an American woman married to a Pole. They did eventually meet up with Anderson and Peterson.

In a publication called the "Canadian Airmen in Poland" 11, 1962 this article was written by Sgt. Peterson.

Sgt Peterson, one of the survivors, wrote about his experiences during this mission in a publication called the "Canadian Airmen in Poland". He described how in the briefing room before take-off, crew members were instructed that the purpose of this flight was no longer a supply mission to Warsaw but instead a meeting and supply drop for the Home Army in the Polish countryside. He reported how the supplies were discharged over the prescribed meeting place and then how the aircraft was attacked by a night fighter. After parachuting from the aircraft Sgt Peterson landed on the side of a hill about 50 feet from a small forest, where he hid his parachute and started running. He heard the barking of dogs and steps of someone coming after him. He described how he ran without stopping, until he finally fell from exhaustion and was able to hide successfully in a field with tall crops.

He explained how the sound of the steps he had heard had been his own heart pounding 'like a hammer'. He remained in this field during the day - and that night knocked on the door of a nearby house. The man of the house opened the door to be confronted by Sgt Peterson in a blue uniform and a pistol in his holster –whereby the man and his family were speechless. Sgt Peterson remembered that they seemed to be filled with terror and were not able to utter a single word. Eventually after talking feverishly among themselves for a while they guessed that he must be a British airman who would be sought by the Germans. Sgt Peterson wrote that he had felt sympathy, concern and compassion from this family - who took care of him while hiding him in their attic. Sgt Peterson and the other survivors eventually served for a time with the AK battalion 'Barbara' 16 pp AK."

F/O Anderson had landed in a field just south of Tarnow. He found safety in a farmhouse where he met up on August 8 with Sgt. Robert Peterson who had landed safely and sought the help of a family. Local partisans had looked after Sgt. Peterson in the Lyczana area and on September 11th Sgt's Charles Underwood and Alan Jolly joined them and they stayed together as a group until September 20, 1944.

As the most senior of the men Flying Officer Phillip Anderson felt responsible to make every possible effort to get them home safely to England. This was no easy task. He did manage at sometime to get a message relayed to Intelligence groups about the fate of JP 162 and its crew and that "four of the crew were safe with Polish partisans and three crew had been KIA". He felt that they should not stay in any one place too long and he tried unsuccessfully to arrange for guides to get them to Czechoslovakia. He met with a commandant of a large group of partisans who had been told to take care of the "British Pilots" and get them through to the Russian Lines. They stayed with the group after avoiding German troops. Phillip Anderson was able to persuade the commandant to find a safer hiding place for them until it was safe to move elsewhere. Eventually they made their way to a farm near Tarnow where they stayed for two weeks hidden in a barn.

The four airmen were forced to split up but in his account given to MI9 Phillip Anderson he felt very uneasy about this decision. Anderson and Underwood stayed together and Peterson and Jolly were together. In reading several accounts of other airmen who were also evading capture it was stated the evading airmen if possible joined together with Canadian airmen who in many cases could speak French. It was thought that this gave the evading airmen a better chance if they were ever stopped and questioned. As both Sgt. Peterson and F/O Anderson were Canadian I wonder if this was part of their strategy when they did finally split into two groups. F/O Anderson and Sgt. Underwood moved to Tarnow about October 15th and were sheltered in a house on Kollataja 9 Street at the Hubert Portachke house where I believe the German High Commissioner often visited. They had been brought to this house by two men thought to be Stanislaw Wodzinski and an unknown priest. Wodzinski was a shop steward in Tarnow knew Hubert Portschke. The airmen were fully aware the great risk the family was taking and were careful to keep wearing their uniforms rather then civilian clothes. The family continued to lead as normal life as possible but few people really knew what went on behind the heavily draped windows. They stayed there until the Russian Army arrived on January 16, 1945. At the time these two airmen were living at this house in Tarnow the Poetschke family was also hiding a young Jewish girl.

On October 5th until the 26th Sgt Jolly and Sgt Peterson were safe in hiding in private peasants houses in Plesna about 15 miles from Tarnow. They were moved once more as the Germans were once again rounding up young men. This time they stayed with another family in Mesna Opacka south of

Tarnow until 25th January 1945. Sgt. Underwood had at one time managed to gain passage and had obtained a document which would give passage on a flight out of Poland for all of them but this proved to be a ruse as no airport existed.

F/O Anderson arranged for Sgt's Jolly and Peterson to be taken by a guide to Tarnow on January 20, 1945. At this point the four airmen would not be together again and each pair would find their own way to find transport back to England.

F/O Anderson continued his brave attempts to get "British Pilots" as they were called by the Polish people back to England. His first encounters with the Soviets were on January 18, 1945 and his accounts in his evasion reports show that he was continually asking them for help. Many of his attempts were ignored but he would sometimes find himself in situations

Robert Peterson (L) & Alan Jolly (R) taken in "Safe House" Tarnow Jan. 1945. Photo courtesy of Agnieszka Partridge.

where he was putting his life in danger when he refused to take no for an answer. Some of the actions he took seemed highly comical especially if the reader is not fully aware of the seriousness of his situation and circumstances.

The Russians kept claiming that they had no ships to send the Allied POWs back across the Black Sea to Southern Europe. The response by the Allied "powers that be" by the lack of aide was quick because they immediately sent a mini-fleet of Allied troop and hospital ships to Odessa. There was a memo sent from the Military Mission in Moscow to the Middle East Headquarters in February 1945 which advised them to take action in getting these men safely home.

Members of all the armed forces including merchant seamen who were from the UK, Canada and Australia were to be shipped home to the UK on the Duchess of Bedford. All men who belonged to forces of the Dominions, Colonies and India were to be sent home via the Middle East on the Morton Bay. Finally anyone from UK, Canada or Australia who had not been able to board the Duchess of Bedford were to sail on the Morton Bay as far as the Middle East where they would join a convey of ships sailing to the UK.

Several hundred airmen and army personnel had found their way to Krakow with the hopes of getting a passage home by train. On February 25, 1945 after eating breakfast, the Russians marched them to the railroad station and there they were put into cattle box cars, 35 men to the smaller cars and 65 in each of the larger ones which was to take them first to Kiev and then to Odessa. They were given hard tack (this was a type of cracker or biscuit, made from flour, water and sometimes salt. It was cheap to make and had as they say today had a long shelf life. The name comes from sailor slang for food, "tack"). The Russians also supplied enough tea for about three meals and some salt pork (fat) and some American Porridge but no utensils to cook it! As an extra they added some bread and sausage. Each of the cars had a small stove but very little fuel. F/O. Anderson in his report to MI9 did make a comment "that the hard tack that they had been given was inedible but it made quite good fuel." The men arrived in Odessa on February 28 after spending six bitterly cold nights on the train. They were then held in a camp until March 7th when they boarded the Morton Bay which would take them to Port Said. The process of the men boarding the ship took a long time as the Russians checked off each man on their list as well as suddenly producing two documents for the Allied authorities to sign. One document stated the number of troops on the ship and that the troops had no complaints against the Soviet Union. The other stated that the Allied authorities would not accept the ten day provisions for the men. Finally this piece of blackmail was resolved and the ship set sail. To add interest to the departure of the Morton Bay two airmen from the crew JP162 were aboard F/O. Anderson and Sgt. Underwood. The Canadian Phillip Anderson was appointed Messing Officer and was helped by two NCOs. There were a total of 1,700 of "all ranks" aboard as they sailed for home.

I believe first meeting that Sgt.'s Jolly and Peterson with the Soviets was when they reported to the Russian War Commandant on February 9th, 1945 at Tarnow. They were given passes to travel to Rzeszow and they met up with Sgt. Walter Davis[37] who had been avoiding capture since April 1944 when his plane JP 224 piloted by Warrant Officer Tom Storey had engine trouble and crashed. Walter Davies had become separated from the rest of his crew. Four of the crew had been helped the Russian partisans and were safely in England within ten weeks, but two others had been captured and had become POWs. Sgt Davis spent over a year trying to return to England first being hidden by a Polish family for five months and then later joining up with a group of Polish partisans where he met Sgt.'s Jolly and Peterson.

Reading the accounts Sgt Davis gave to MI9 and later his written recollections of these events made me aware that even those who were able to evade being captured by the Germans were living a life were they were in constant danger. Later Sgt's Davis, Jolly and Peterson and other evading airmen went by train to Odessa and then boarded the ship Duchess of Bedford on March 14th, 1945 to take them first to Malta where they boarded the liner Orion. Sgt Davis calls this ship "a fine liner" but it was a troop ship and instead of having the luxury of cabins as that had had on the Duchess of Bedford they had to go down to the troop deck but as he pointed out "that was the least of our worries, we were on our way home[38]."

They then sailed to Gibraltar, where a convoy of ships was formed the Orion becoming the Commodore ship of the convoy. It is said that when the captain, who I believe was Polish, discovered that there were three airmen on board Peterson, Jolly and Davies who had been part of the Polish partisan group he ordered them to his cabin and ordered his aide to bring the airmen an ale. This was against regulations but the captain felt that this regulation should be broken because of the unusual circumstance. The men I am sure appreciated the kind gesture. They were finally on their way home!

On their return all the airmen were interviewed by MI9 and gave full reports of the attack of their aircraft, their evasion tactics and the help that they received from the Polish people and the partisan groups. According to 148 Squadrons record book for August 5, 1944 the comments written by the squadrons diarist in the report read as follows:

"This disastrous night robbed the squadron of both "A" and "B" flight Commanders and left only one officer pilot (F/L R.G. N. Pryor) who took control of the 2 Flights. In addition we now have only four serviceable aircraft and one fully effective crew who have only 11 hours flying time before they complete their tour. The absence of even a nucleus of experienced crews gravely affected the work of the Squadron throughout the month, as did the fact that speedy replacement for the aircraft we had lost was not forthcoming."[34]

After the war ended, Air Marshall Sir John Slessor in several speeches he made stated how troubled he that he had to make so many agonizing decisions during the war. He had taken the heavy losses very much to heart and stated that "this was the worst six weeks of my war time career" and apologized for his part in sending these aircrews on such dangerous missions.

In 2007 F/L Pryor recalled in a letter he sent to the Warsaw Uprising Museum that "this was not one of the squadron's better nights", a masterpiece of British understatement. This proved to be one of the most disastrous missions that RAF 148 Squadron would undertake and the losses over the coming weeks of August and September would reach a staggering 265 airmen sacrificed.

The Airlift failed in trying to aid the Polish people but it served to cement the bond between the Poles and the allied forces that had helped. The Polish people have never forgotten the sacrifice that these airmen from Britain, Canada, Australia, and South Africa made.

CHAPTER 14

AFTERMATH

The heavy loss of crews and aircraft meant the families at home had to be notified about the fate of their loved ones. I am concerned particularly with the crew my father's plane but three other aircraft dispatched on the 4/5th August had also "failed to return." It was virtually impossible to determine the whereabouts and condition of their crews as no news had reached Brindisi. Each Halifax had a crew of seven airmen so there were twenty eight families who had to be informed which was made more difficult because of the secrecy of these missions. In most cases telegrams would be sent informing the families that their son or husband, father or brother was "missing in action." When further news was heard the telegram would be revised to a different status POW, Evader, or the worst possible news killed in action, (KIA).

My mother, Alice, along with the next of kin of the crew of JP162 was one of those families to receive such a telegram telling her the plane and airmen were missing. It is impossible to imagine what my mother must have felt when she received the news that her husband John was missing. I have often wondered if she was with family or might she have been alone? How do you survive such news? Although the first telegram said missing Alice Rae at the age of 28 was now in all probability a widow with a three month old baby girl to care for. What was her life going to be like? The waiting for further news must have been agonizing. Not knowing if her husband John was alive or dead, the days waiting for further news must have been endless. The telegram had simply stated:

"I regret to inform you that you husband Sgt. John F.C. Rae has been reported missing. Any further information will be communicated to you immediately".

The delays in getting information were inevitable given the difficulties in which the surviving crew found themselves in Poland. She would later receive a letter form the Commanding Officer of 148 Squadron and probably much later another letter from the Air Ministry[39] telling her the about the report from Flying Officer P.J. Anderson RACF the navigator on her husbands plane when he finally returned to Britain in March 1945. The report "that three of the crew had been KIA!" One of those three was her husband John, my dad.

Four of the families of the JP162 crew would eventually receive good news but mum and the families of James McCall and Clifford Aspinall received the very worst possible news that there loved ones would never be returning home.

Like many families the only loss to the families of the airmen who did not return was simply represented by just three medals. First the 1939-1945 Star, the Aircrew Europe Star (in my dads case the Italian Star) and the British War Medal which arrived in a small brown cardboard box and delivered by the Post Office addressed to the next of kin , my mother. These medals had attached a commendation stating who they were awarded to but the medals themselves were not engraved as it was thought too expensive to do so by the government at that time.

As I write about this sad time I have nothing but the deepest love and respect for my mum. In those very difficult circumstances she was able to push her sadness aside and began to make a new life for the two of us.

Alice and Rosemary 1947

She had bought a small house in Morecambe and made a new home just for us. She was always a very creative person and a very "good manager" so we were happy as we could be settling into our new surrounding. My mum Lal also had the help of her wider family as we still be living in the same town plus the constant support of my dad's younger sister Margaret and her husband Charlie "Uncle Charlie my hero". They helped my mum in so many ways and were always there to help when needed and gave support in raising me on the days when my mum was unable to. My first few years were divided between my home in Morecambe and theirs in Helensburgh. This was not a sad time because I lived surrounded by lots of love from people who loved both my mum and I very much.

When I was about three years old my mum Alice Rae decided to move to a small town just outside Glasgow on the River Clyde to be near her sister-in-law Margaret. The town was Helensburgh which was only a few miles from where my dad had grown up. It must have been a major decision for her to make but one I suspect was the right one for her at that time.

Moving day arrived and one of my earliest memories is sitting on one of the tea chests which the removal company had brought to the house to pack up our belongings. My mother had bought a house overlooking the River Clyde in Helensburgh. It is a house that I remember with great fondness. As usual she "set to" to get the necessary work done to make it a comfortable home painting and decorating, sewing curtains. She worked to get the house just as she wanted it. Once she had the inside of our home the way she liked she set about working on designing and planning the garden. She had as the saying goes "a green thumb." The design took shape and rose bushes were planted as well as perennials. One of her favorite places to visit was the nursery garden in a small town called Rhu not too far from our home. We didn't have a car so we would walk through the beautiful tree lined streets. Helensburgh is laid out in a grid system with wide pavements and grass verges. In spring the streets which were lined with Cherry blossom trees were in full bloom and daffodils flowered in the grass verges. It was magical. She would order her plants and bulbs for the next season and they would be delivered. In winter because the town was on a hill these same streets were ideal for sledding.

As always my two favorite relatives, Auntie Margaret and Uncle Charlie were always around to provide additional help. My mum had finished most of the work she could do but she needed to have some cupboards built and along came Andrew. Andrew was a skilled carpenter who set about working and building the cupboards she needed. Eventually she and Andrew married and I was part of a family once again though I never took his surname as my mother insisted that I remain a RAE.

We were a happy family and through "my dad" I gained a whole new set of uncle's, aunts and grandparents. The word "step" in front of "dad" was never used. He and his family treated me with lots of love and kindness. My father John Rae, as Andrew had also known him, was never forgotten and was talked about often. Looking back I wished I had asked more questions but as a child, life is forever and there is always tomorrow Life was good! As an only child perhaps I was spoiled but I always felt secure. My mum was not always in the best of health but Andrew, as I now call him, took me on lots of trips. Trips on the paddle steamers Waverly and Jeannie Deans down the Clyde to Dunoon and Rothsey. We took trips by train to Edinburgh to visit the castle and the zoo and also to Ayr to visit Robert

Burns's cottage and long bike rides through Glen Fruin. I remember them all as if it were yesterday.

At home I would sit on the widow seat, which Andrew had built, in my bedroom and watch the ocean liners Empress of Canada and Empress of Scotland dock at Greenock and set sail for a far off place called Canada. I saw famous ships such as the Mauritania make their last journey to the breakers yard at Faslane sounding her mournful horns. At that time there was, as there still is today, the Royal Navy submarine base on the Gareloch at Faslane. In spring there were the bluebell woods to visit and in summer the tide pools along the shore to explore. I spent many hours alone but I was content and I always had something to keep me busy.

There were rare but special trips with my mum on the train to Glasgow where we would visit the large department stores for special outfits for Easter, usually a dress or suit complete with hat and gloves. No young lady or grown woman would be seen without these two important accessories. One year I had heard my friends talk about a wonderful department store called C&A so I persuaded my mum to take me there for my Easter outfit. She was not at all impressed and thought the clothes looked "cheap and not well finished." I on the other hand thought differently. They were stylish and modern looking and I picked out a suit. My mum gave in and to this day that was one of my favorite outfits which I wore and wore. On one of our shopping trips to Glasgow my mum took me to the cinema to see a film she wanted to see. This was a rare treat as we didn't go to the cinema very often. This cinema was different. On the upper balcony instead of rows of seats it had small tables covered with linen cloths with small table lamps and comfortable chairs and afternoon tea was served while we watched the picture. This was a very special memory and I can even remember the film "A Man Called Peter."

**The last picture taken of Alice Rae and her
daughter Rosemary 1957**

I attended the Hermitage Primary School and later Hermitage Academy. I was not always a good scholar but I was always trying hard to do my best to make everyone proud.

In 1948 there was great excitement when my baby cousin Ian was born. My Auntie Margaret and Uncle Charlie had on Christmas Day 1938 lost their only son Robert at the age of two. They had applied to adopt a baby and Ian was brought to them just a few hours after he was born. We were all so happy and knew that this tiny baby would be loved and would bring much joy to his parents and to all of us. He became a really special part of my life.

As I grew older I would travel to visit my Grandparents and Aunt in Morecambe and as I remember I would always travel

First Class and be "put in charge of the guard" on the train, much as children in America fly (called unaccompanied minor) and are now put in charge of the aircraft cabin staff to make even longer journeys in this vast country. People were so trusting.

I remember one day my mum received a letter from the Commonwealth War Grave Commission. My dad Sergeant John Rae had been buried by the villagers in a village called Wojnarowa and now the Commission had moved his remains and those of the other crew members to Krakow where the graves could be formally and taken care of.

Letters had been sent to all the families who had lost a loved one. With them was a questionnaire and the information from these was compiled and entered into ledgers which are kept in a small box at the entrance of each of the War Graves Commission cemeteries. Sadly the upheaval of the war and post war period meant that many of these letters never reached the families. Many had moved and many of them simply decided not to respond. The letter also asked my mother if she would like an inscription on her husband's headstone. I remember my mum trying to decide what words she would like inscribed on his gravestone. I am sure this must have brought up a lot of sadness and questions. She decided on very simple message:

Treasured Memories

Loving Thoughts

Lal and Rosemary.

I recalled vividly that moment fifty years later in 1994 when I was able to visit Krakow. I stood by his headstone and there the words were. For many years travel to Poland was difficult so my mum was never able to make that journey. I made it for her.

Life in Helensburgh continued happily until was once again tragedy struck not once but twice the first tragedy occurring in July 1958 and another in November of the same year. On July 4th my Aunt Margaret and Uncle Charlie's young son Ian was killed, he was just ten years old. It was on a hot evening; July 4th Ian had ridden his bike to buy an ice cream. We were all heartbroken. Ian and I were close. He would always be waiting at his primary schoolyard for me on the days I would go to his school for some of my classes, such a sweet boy. His home was always a happy place to visit and I had spent so much time there when I was growing up that it became my second home. Without Ian there it was not the same but I spent time with my aunt and uncle. They were so sad, as was my mother, I continued to visit and went back to school with a heavy heart after the summer holidays because this year there would be no Ian to meet me.

Six months later on November 6th another tragedy. It was the week before my school exams, I was struggling and as much as I tried to study it's as if I was staring at a blank page, I just could not retain anything I was reading. My dad Andrew was working on part of the house they were making into a separate apartment and my mum had still not come home from her work at the sub-post office. I put on my coat and decided to walk to the nearby bus stop in the hopes I would meet her arriving but as bus pulled in no mum. I waited for the next bus. No passengers got off. I decided to call in at Andrew's parent's home because she sometimes stopped on her way home. They lived just three houses away. My mum was there but there was lots of confusion because she had become ill. No one had tried to find Andrew or me. I was mad and ran home to tell him and we raced back to see what was happening. They had taken my mum upstairs to lie down till she felt better. I don't know if anyone had even thought to call her doctor or even call the emergency number. Of course something was obviously wrong and it seemed very little was being done to help her. A cousin was sent for and

I was taken to spend the night with her. When I thought about this afterwards there are many questions "why didn't they just take me to my Aunt Margaret and Uncle Charlie they would know what to do and make things better." I didn't sleep. I kept wondering what was happening? Why would they make me leave? That question would be answered in the morning when I was told that my mum had died. Of course now that many years have passed since that event then I realize the people present should have sent for the emergency services and her doctor as soon as she became ill even if the outcome was the same.

How could life be so cruel to take two people who I loved so much? What was to become of me? I was fourteen and lost, totally and utterly lost.

The next days are a blur. Two days later my mother's funeral was held. I remember sitting with my Aunt Margaret and Uncle Charlie after I attended the service but not the burial which I was not allowed to attend. Aunt Margaret said some strange words: "This is meant to be Rosemary. We are meant to be together." I wondered what she meant and it wasn't until my mothers will was read that I realize what had been said was not going to be as Margaret wished. A second blow had been struck. I was to live with my mum's older sister Annie and her family and my grandparents many miles away in Morecambe where I had been born. Less than a week later from that awful day my life changed utterly and drastically and I moved away from the town and people who I loved and who loved me. There seemed to be no time for me to collect together some mementos of my mum, pictures and her special box of treasured possessions she had of my dad, my books and small tokens that would remind me of all the happy times. Maybe deep down I thought that I would return. Andrew and I did not seem to be able to have any time together. He was grieving for his wife and now the little girl he had helped raise was leaving.

John Rae's sister Margaret and her husband Charlie, two favorite people in the authors life.

Because of circumstances best left unsaid and the fact that Andrew had never adopted me and had no parental rights I lost all contact with him and I was not brave enough to stand up to defend him. One couple did not give up, my dad's younger sister Margaret and her husband. No matter what, they were always there for me even if was often from a distance. At the age of 14 I had no say in the matter of with whom and where I was to live and I was never asked. I would have told everyone exactly where I wanted to be. I can't dwell on the negatives suffice to say that life to me was never quite the same even though I lived with people who cared for me. Even though I lived in a busy household there never seemed to be anyone to talk to so I often felt very alone. I realize now that we were all grieving. My grandparents for their daughter, my aunt for her sister and my cousin for his favorite aunt he had also loved, and I for my mum. Instead of trying to help each other and grieve together we each grieved alone.

I was now back in the town were I had been born, Morecambe. In its heyday in the 1950's and early 1960's during the summer months it was a place where people who lived in the industrial towns and cities would come for a week's holiday. The many theatres were alive with variety shows featuring the popular artists of the day. The big bands played in the ballroom on the Central Pier. There was ballroom dancing every morning and afternoon to the Wurlitzer organ at the Winter Gardens Ballroom and the town boasted one of the largest swimming pools with the weekly beauty contest for Miss Great Britain. Landaus with their well groomed horses waited patiently to take visitors on a ride along the seafront. Coaches would take guests on day excursions or in the evening on a "Mystery Tour" and of course the ever popular noisy fairground rides and slot machines. It was all happening plenty to do and see as long as the sun was shining. Gradually people became more adventurous and began taking their holidays abroad in Spain where for an all inclusive price they could have two weeks of 'fun in the sun" and sadly this began the decline of Morecambe and many of the seaside resorts in England.

Life somehow returned to normalcy and arrangements were made for me to return to school in the hopes that my mind would be kept occupied with settling into a new school and hopefully making friends. It was decided that I should attend the Girls Grammar School in Lancaster which would be a bus ride from home. I knew from the first day I sat in the 2nd year's class that this was not the place for me and a few weeks later I was back at home with a very angry aunt now trying to decide what she should do next. She did not think the local secondary school, a short walk from home, was suitable. Enlisting the help of a friend who taught at a girl's school in Lancaster, which had in those days a good reputation, a meeting was arranged with the Headmistress and I found myself back on the bus journeying to Lancaster this time in the 4th Year class. In all this mix up and because of the different schooling systems in England and Scotland somehow I had lost a year of schooling. Settling in as best I could some friendships were made. One in particular friendship was to reunite me with someone who I had last shared a special day many years ago on May 7h 1944. Her name was Amy Lowe and as she had been telling her parents about "a new girl joining her class" and mentioned my name her parents showed her a church magazine which showed we had been christened on the same day at St Johns Church, Heysham. Sadly this friendship did not last as Amy and her entire family was involved in a horrific crash and was killed as they drove on their summer holiday the following year. Little did I realize that many years later I would meet two sisters who had also attended this same school? The rest of the friendships I made in those early days were superficial. Everyone was interested in why I was now living with an aunt and grandparents but their curiosity was curbed by parents telling them that it was not their business and not to ask questions. I believe in many ways questions would have been better than silence.

At this time a lady from the Ministry of Pensions entered the picture. Her name was Miss McGrath, a large, very kindly Irish lady who visited me often both at home and at school and later was instrumental in making sure I had the funds for college. As my dad had died during his RAFVR service my mother and then I were eligible to receive a War pension from the Government. Miss McGrath was there to help me in any way she could. She took care of me until I finished my teacher training course in Manchester and started my first teaching job and at that time no longer eligible to receive a pension. She was quite proud of the fact that I was one of the few surviving children who were still receiving this "war pension" in the mid 1960s.

I lived with my mothers sister; not always happily, for the next seven years. I finished my schooling by attending a local College of Further Education and found a City and Guilds Course in Home Economics and Home Management that I enjoyed and excelled and was able to continue by completing the teacher training part of the course in Manchester. I was proud of my achievements and found a teaching position in the south of England in Slough. I became a respected member of the teaching staff at a secondary school and was finally living on my own enjoying life. This was my first real achievement and accomplishment especially when the head of the woodwork department who had been teaching for many years came to ask me, a first year teacher, if I would please take one of his students who he could no longer cope with. John Mumford (I still remember his name) became the first boy to join a cookery class and he became one of my best students. My head of department was very impressed. I was extremely happy teaching.

During my second year of teaching I was able to buy a small car called an Austin Mini. I was lucky enough to be reunited with my mother's youngest brother Sam and his family and I met my future husband Robert through their daughter Barbara my cousin. Robert's parents and his sister Mary welcomed me and made me feel very much at home and part of their family whenever I visited, which was often. We became engaged a few months later and the following summer we were married. This of course meant that I had to leave my teaching post and find a new job as we would be living in Chatham, Kent.

Life was good. Lots of new adventures in setting up our home together and Robert settled into his new job as an aerospace engineer after gaining his degree at London University. I wasn't so lucky with my move to a new school and after a couple of terms I left and secured what turned out to be my "dream job" working in a small secondary school with a great group of teachers and students. It was located in a small village just outside Maidstone, Kent where we would settle and buy our first home. It was here that I remembered my star pupil John Mumford as I set about organizing a Boys After School Cookery Club with the full support of my head of department and the Headmaster. This venture turned out to be a great success.

A couple of years later we had our first daughter Michelle and I took some time away from teaching. It was a happy time for everyone and Robert's parents were delighted to welcome their first grandchild and my former students were always pleased to be able to baby sit. When Michelle was two I got a call form my school headmaster and was asked if I could come and cover for a colleague who would be away for about a term. What was I to do with my daughter and was told to "bring her too!!" This was a rural school which had a small farm attached and while I had been away raising my daughter a new complex of buildings to house woodwork, metal shop and home economics departments was being built. A small nursery school was planned for the older students to learn child care. It was an exciting opportunity to be asked to help and so each morning for the next few weeks we walked to school and I was back doing something I loved.

Michelle was taken care of by the girls who were taking their child care classes and the boys would take her to visit the animals on the farm and their teacher "Uncle Bill". When the teacher for whom I was taking care of her classes returned I was offered a part time teaching post. What was most exciting part of all this was the fact that girls were now offered classes in woodwork and metalwork and the boy's home economics all this stemming form my Boys Cookery Club and that troubled student John Mumford!

Eventually there came a time for Robert to seek promotion and we were again on the move. Our youngest daughter Helen was born, our oldest daughter Michelle started school and the years saw us moving north and settling in Lytham St Annes.

Our biggest and most challenging move came in 1980. Not just a few miles this time but a move across an ocean and continent to the west coast of the United States to a small town called Kirkland on Lake Washington, just outside Seattle. Family and friends were at a loss as to where we were headed then an event occurred which would tell then exactly where we were headed. In May, 1980 Mt St Helens erupted! Not far from where we were going to live.

It was an exciting adventure and our neighbors on the cal de sac where we had rented a house welcomed us on their Independence Day July 4th, 1980 by taking us to see a fireworks display. The girls settled into school, my husband was happy working at Boeing Airplane Company and eventually he was asked to become a permanent employee. There was much discussion and we decided to make America our home in many ways like the Rae brothers had done so many years ago. We enjoyed our new opportunities and settled well into everyday life by buying our first home. Life was good but families back in England were quite sad that we had decided to stay.

In 1984 our move to California came when a promotion and job offer came Robert's way. We settled in a small community called Camarillo where the girls would be able to attend school. Robert would have a longer commute to work a hundred mile round trip each day but eventually when the girls were grown and had left home we would have the opportunity to move and settle nearer to his work.

We are happy, the girls are married and settled and we have welcomed our four grandsons, a Californian, two Texas boys and later a little boy from Arkansas, the next generation.

Somehow the years have slipped by and there are times when something will remind me of those days long ago. The good memories return such as hearing a song I remember my mother singing so long ago. She had a wonderful singing voice and would often sing as she was busy working around the house. The other day I heard someone singing a beautiful lilting melody. "Just a Song at Twilight" which was popular in the early 1900's and a picture of my mother singing this came to mind. She had probably heard my grandfather sing this when she was growing up. It is strange that even today I still remember some special moments which happened so long ago. I think those memories made us who we were and who we became.

After more then forty five years in the aerospace industry Robert retired in 2013. Life is different and at a slower pace but looking back we are still glad that we made that major decision to move to America all those years ago.

For most of these years of marriage I have counted myself very fortunate to have been able to stay at home while the girls were in school and to have had time to follow and trace my family history. In family life everyone has happiness and sadness but I feel very lucky.....but the tragedies and mysteries of my early life were ever present. My trip to Krakow in 1994, although healing in some respects had left me wanting to know more, not least about my fathers background. It took me on a journey to trace my roots and find out who I was. Not always an easy road to travel, many twists and turns and bumps in the road but one I am so pleased to have had the opportunity to make. Life wasn't always a bed of roses. There were thorns too but overtime I feel that I overcame the unhappy and sad times and people in my life who did not make things easy.

This year 2014 is a year for remembrance and for looking back and also looking to the future. It is 70 years since my family went from the utter joy of happy celebrations to the depths of despair of a tragic event but it was also a year that we as a family survived and grew stronger. Deep down if truth be known I am a Rae through and through and as I have learned through this "Special Journey" we are tough and resilient lot.

I am proud to say I am my father's daughter and my mother's too!!!

PART TWO

MY JOURNEY TO KRAKOW

CHAPTER 15

THE LONG ROAD TO KRAKOW

In March, 2012 I felt that I had collected together all the available information I could on Halifax JP162FS-s and its aircrew. I put the information in order in my files and was quite pleased with what I had been able to collect over the years. It had not been an easy task. I had started with very little information that I had built with the pictures, letters and documents that my dad's younger sister Margaret had given me several years ago which I had been able to use as a starting point and build on them.

Little did I realize that an email I would receive a few weeks later would find me opening my files and the following year find me planning a visit to Krakow to meet with complete strangers?

The message was from Paul Frazier who is the grandson of Flt. Lt James Girvan McCall RAFVR the pilot of Halifax JP 162FS-S for sugar the very plane that my dad Sgt John Rae RAFVR had flown on as an Air Gunner. It was a total shock. I had been searching for the other airmen (or their families) who were on JP 162's last flight on August 4/5 1944 for such a long time and it was hard to believe that after all these years someone connected to this plane had finally answered.

Hi Rosemary,

I saw your posts on from April 2007. I am the grandson of James Girvan McCall, or Girvan as I believe he was know by.

Do you have any further information, the only real details I can find are - Girvan's wife, my Grandmother, Catherine is now 93. My mother (Eileen), who was only 3 months old when Girvan died, is now 68. Sadly, I believe Girvan only saw my mum once, due to his postings with the RAF.

Regards
Paul Fraser.

The McCall family is still living in Edinburgh. James McCall or Girvan as his family called him was the pilot and one of the aircrew who was killed on that fatal last mission of JP 162. In 1944 he was just 23. His widow Catherine though still alive is in frail health, as might be expected for someone in her nineties. His daughter Eileen is about the same age as me and like me was only seen once by her father before he was killed. I was thrilled to be able to respond and share with him the information I had collected over the years. Now I was in a quandary "what to do?" The research I thought I had completed was pulling me in again and I did not know whether or not to take it further.

Needless to say I found myself searching for more information about RAF 148 Squadron and by chance on of my searches lead to a Website called "Operation Dark of the Moon" which had been founded by Terry Marker. This was a site which had not existed when I first began my research. The site is devoted to the history of 148 Squadron and it contributors all have some connection through a family member or friends who either served or have some attachment to the squadron. Everyone is interested in a specific timeframe so with everyone's information imputed the site is a treasure trove of information about all things 148.

I was welcomed to the group and very quickly expanded my knowledge of JP 162FS and its aircrew. Many unanswered questions were answered and in many ways I was overwhelmed with all this new information. Paul Frasier had also given me a link to a website remembering the crews of downed aircraft and here I gained more information about the crash site. The file I thought was closed was getting thicker. The year 2012 was also a special year in the United Kingdom. Queen Elizabeth 11 was celebrating her Diamond Jubilee after sixty years on the throne. That same year a memorial to Bomber Command was finally to be dedicated so there was much written about the "brave young men" who served with Bomber Command during WW2. My sister-in-law Mary sent me some great information and DVD's of TV programs that had been shown in Britain.

It is at this stage a young man from Krakow Robert Reichert enters the picture. In some of my searches I had come across some stunning pictures he had posted of the Allied Section at Rakowicki Cemetery in Krakow, Poland. This was the first time that I became aware that these brave men who are buried so far away from home had never been forgotten by the people of Krakow. His pictures showed some of the graves of the Blynn and Crabtree crews who had been lost on the same mission as my father August 4/5th 1944. I contacted Robert and the rest "you can say is history." Not only did he visit Rakowicki and take some newer pictures he became my researcher, my translator and a really good friend.

I had been trying to find the person whose house was built on the site of the JP 162 crash as well the Polish TV crew who had made a documentary in 2010 of the excavation of the site but without success and suddenly Robert gave me exactly the information I needed. I contacted the owner a Josef Koszyk by mail and received a wonderful reply. Josef then contacted his friend Tomak Jastrzębski an aircraft historian who had been involved in the excavation. Tomasz sent me a letter saying he was so pleased to hear about my connection to JP 162 and they also contacted the Home Army Museum. The next letter I received was from Robert Springwald the curator of the

Home Army Museum in Krakow. All the while Robert Reichert continued to find interesting pieces of information which included a copy of a Polish TV Documentary which in 2010 had covered the excavation of Halifax JP162 in the village of Niecew. All of these were interesting pieces of information which began to fill in the many blanks.

My friends at Operation Dark of the Moon were full of encouragement and member Piotr Hoydra from Poland was able to give me a full account of my dad's service and the operations he and his crew flew with 148 Special Duties Squadron out of Brindisi after I had struggle for so long trying to get this information from sources in England. I was sent more information about the four airmen who survived and who spent months in safe houses and marching with the AK Army. Some of this information seemed so unreal but later when I was contacted by a Kris and Agnieszka Partridge another dimension to the story was added and the facts I had were confirmed as true.

In March 2013, I made a trip to England and was able to gain some valuable information form the National Archives at Kew. These were the 148 Squadron Operations Record Books and Evaders reports. I was able to read the squadron records of all the flights that my dad had made with his crew on all those long missions. I was also able to read and get copies of the accounts that the four airmen had given to MI9 on their return to England after their long struggle to return. It was also surprising to find that some of this wealth of information came from the least expected places and people.

And so began the planning of my journey to Krakow. I wanted to be in Krakow on August 4 and 5th 2013 so I could be there on the 69th anniversary of the Warsaw Uprising. I wanted to visit my dad's grave and those of his crew plus pay respects to the other airmen who had lost their lives so long ago. I built my visits around those dates and Tomasz Jastrzębski took time off work and delayed his vacation and started panning a full week of wonderful events which came as a complete surprise when we finally arrived. Plans were made and all these special people who I had contact with during the past months were waiting for my arrival in Krakow. It was hard to believe that I few months ago I had closed my files. Now because of one random email I was now ready to make the long journey to Krakow.

LETTERS TO AND FROM POLAND

There were many letters to and from Poland. Information came from Robert Reichert of Krakow who posted some stunning pictures on All Saints Day 2010 at Rakowicki Cemetery. He wrote a wonderful tribute to the crew of JP 162. As I said earlier he has become my source of information and my translator and a wonderful friend. His pictures can be found throughout this story.

Subject: Rakowicki Cemetery
Date: 26th October, 2012

Hello Rosemary,
I'm going to visit the Rakowicki Cemetery on All Saints Day or All Souls Day next week, so if only I am there I will certainly visit your father's grave too. I can't be however sure of the time of my visit, so I can't promise night photos. Some parts of the cemetery are hardly accessible when it's dark. I will let you know!

No need to repay in any way of course, I will be happy to do you the favour.

Best regards,
Robert

November 1, 2012.

Hi Rosemary,

I'm happy I was able to do that for you and that I could visit the cemetery after sunset when it looks particularly moving. The All Saints Day and the following All Souls Day are very special religious holidays in Poland, and every visit to Rakowicki Cemetery is unforgettable experience. As you can see in the pictures, a lot of people visit the war cemetery too to light the candles for the fallen soldiers. They rest far from their homes, but have not been forgotten. I was standing there for a while looking at all those tombstones and lights... a very poignant feel.

You may want to know that I posted the photo of your father's grave at flickr with a note with the information about his last flight:

Kind regards,
Robert

Hi Robert

I have just opened the e mail you sent with all those wonderful pictures you took.
I am speechless and have shed a few tears there are not enough words to express my gratitude
I will send another email later
"Lest we forget"
Rosemary

Robert's reply:

Rosemary, I want to tell you that it's a nice feeling to read those letters. They show very well how great job you've already done. I'm sure your visit in Niecew/Wojnarowa villages will be appropriate crowning of your efforts and all the research. I know that you've done all this work both from your own inner need and also in commemoration of your father. And your goal certainly will be reached, because not only for me, but also for many other people involved, your father's grave in the Rakowicki Cemetery won't be just another British grave from the time of the WWII. We will know the real man who was buried here, and we will remember his story!

If I'm only in Krakow at the turn of July and August, I would certainly like to meet you at the cemetery on the anniversary of the JP-162 crash to pay my respect for the fallen airmen.

Robert

LETTERS TO POLAND

Dear Mr. Koszyk,

I have learned that a Polish TV documentary was made by Mr. Adam Sikorski in 2010 about the crash of a Halifax plane JP162FS-S in the village of Wojnarowa on August 4/5th 1944. I believe the site was excavated and some artifacts found.

JP 162 was returning to Brindisi, Italy after dropping supplies to the Polish partisans during the Warsaw Uprising and was attacked and shot down.

My father Sgt. John F C Rae, RAFVR, 148 Special Duties Squadron was the rear gunner on that plane and he was killed along with the pilot Ft Lt James McCall RAFVR and the Upper Gunner Sgt. Clifford Aspinall, RAFVR. Four of the crew managed to bale out and with the help of various groups finally returned buried my father and the other crew who died and later they were re interred at Krakow Rackowicki Cemetery.

I have been able to visit Krakow many years ago but at that time had no knowledge where JP162 had crashed. I have since researched my fathers Royal Air Force Volunteer Reserve service and have gained a great deal more information. Sadly I did not know my father. I was three months old when he died but by trying to find out as much as I can, I am in my way, keeping his memory alive.

I now live in California and I am planning a visit next August to Krakow and to Wojnarowa to coincide with the anniversary of August 4/5th. I hope to be able to meet with the people from your village and maybe gain some more information and also to express my heartfelt gratitude to the villagers who took care of my father and his crew who lost their lives so many years ago. This was not only an act of great kindness but great courage which I will never forget. I hope that you will be able to understand my letter and maybe be able to help me further in collecting more information about JP 162

I look forward to hearing from you.

Kind regards,

Rosemary Edmeads nee Rae

Reply from Josef Koszyk of Niecew, Lesser Poland.

Translation from Polish:

12/12/2012

Hello Ms.

Writing to us gave us a huge surprise for you and much joy. The area still lives in older people who remember World War II times English and shot the plane. The house where my family is, during the construction took out a lot of parts of the plane that killed Mrs. Father. In 2010, around the house were carried out archaeological work, and recovered parts of the aircraft along with transferred by me, after maintenance have been placed in the National Army Museum in Krakow. Fragments JP162 aircraft have constant exposure in the same museum. Work is also preparation for the commemoration of space flight JP162 shooting. Mrs. I allowed myself to address the museum pass, which will get you a lot information on the aircraft and pilots. Regards, Joseph and his family.

We will definitely have to correspond with each other.

Letter from Tomasz Jastrzebski a friend of Josef Koszyk who took part in the excavation of JP 162 in 2010.

My name is Tomasz Jastrzębski and I live in Poland in Wieliczka. With enormous joy and surprising I have accepted message from Mr. Józef Koszyk from Niecew about your letter concerning the Halifax 162 FS-S with 148 Squadron RAF crashed in night 4/5 August 1944 on border of locality Niecew and Wojnarowa . I am chief of group occupying search of place of plane crash and fates of members crews from times of World War II. It has become so happily, that among many others, history of aircraft your dad were object of our research history. Effect of our work was two episodes of historic program TVP entitled: "Było nie minęło". At least you observed one of them! It makes me happy more, that owing to our passion, you can, inform about circumstances of last flights of your Dad.

Found remains are present are important exhibition in museum of National Army in Crakow. There is it symbolic more, because your dad's crew flew with assistance for troops AK. The museum is located next to cemetery where your father has been buried.

We try to take care of memory of great people bearing assistance other not looking for personal life. We are admiration for these young people, who tried to bear in assistance almost suicidal missions. Flying night, solitary, over whole Europe almost unprotected aircraft , searching tiny blazing point , in the area of completely unknown country on which they had to bring down carried away on board load. Load which should help unknown and foreign people in achievement it, what is the most important...the freedom!

Over year ago we have organized great exhibition devoted airmen of RAF, USAAF, and of course PAF. Dramatic history of your dads crew, it was exhibited on it. In our plans is also exhibiting and commemorating on place of catastrophe Halifax FS-S in Niecew. I hope, that. We achieve it with alignment of owner territory Mr. Koszyk.

I am really enjoy, that you want to visit Poland. I hope that we will meet each other and together common visits these important places for you and for us If you will have some notes or wishes concerning visit in Poland, please write to us and we will try to achieve it. On the other hand if it is possible I have a great request about any materials with your dad concerning, especially in RAF service it can be a documents and photos. I will send on you mails photos concerning work archeological in Niecew. if you wish we can send too DVD with recorded programs about this history.

I am apologized for language but my letter was translated by my son because my English is not really good. If you have someone who knew both language I can write in Polish. I will be quicker.

Yours sincerely

Tomasz Jastrzębski

Robert Springwald Krakow 22.01.2013

Madam Rosemary Edmeads

Thank you for the beautiful and informative letter on the crew of Halifax Niecew - Wojnarowa. Together with Tomasz Jastrzebski and a group of aviation history enthusiasts began efforts to honor the crew medals.

Thank you for your courage and willingness to help the Army soldiers who fought in Poland that you father and many of his colleagues paid for life. We invite you to visit the Army Museum. I am very pleased that we will be able to welcome Ms. Krakow.

So far, we have taken the following actions:

First At a meeting in Upper Volunteers 16 December 2012 aviation enthusiasts gathered there resolved to launch efforts to honor the crew medals.

Second Prepared and submitted the appropriate information in documents: UK military attaché, the President's Office and the Council for the Protection of Monuments of Struggle and Martyrdom 3rd All institutions were willing to lend us support and willingness to cooperate in this effort 4th Municipal authorities will take a resolution supporting the the basic information which is necessary for the submission of applications is to address people living (if they exist) or places of burial and contacts to their families or relatives. Without it, nothing can be done.

A great need for family contact details of all the members of the crew. We will do our best to make our state a success.

Robert Springwald.

Letter Sent by Robert Springwald and Aircraft Historians
Group Trying to Get Recognition for the Airmen on JP162

Office of Personnel and Distinctions
Chancellery of the Polish President
ul. Countryside 10
00-902 Warszawa

Office worker thank you very much to me that she found the
time and wanted to take the initiative of a group of materials on
the history of aviation enthusiasts working with Army Museum
in Krakow.

One of the fruits of the exhibition Fri "In the air on the air,"
held at the Museum of Army was awarding two deserving
Airmen: Maj. Anthony Tomiczek - doyen of Polish Air Force
(living in Poland) flying with supplies to Polish and Specera Felt
pilot of U.S. Air Force aircraft, the Bomber War II in horses
World crashed in Upper Volunteers.

We have taken the initiative to reward the next crew. First of all
we would like to honor foreigners (they fly freely without
motivation patriotic) the first plane will be the crew of the RAF
Halifax Wojnarowej. This is an airplane that we studied. The
initiative planned for many years.

To bear the loss of the crew flying to Poland the discharges
were enormous.

After the war (for obvious reasons) there was not a possibility,
nor the will to honor these soldiers. In fact, the graves of
airmen buried in the cemetery Rakowicki should be sufficient to
justify the request. Those people without any connection with
the Polish voluntarily gave their life.

We would like to interest you in this initiative and look forward to working.

After collecting all the data relevant applications will be filed in the Office of the President

Robert Springwald

Memory Lane

Craig Fleming with our Tuesday and Saturday nostalgia pages.

Celebrate the Fylde

This Day

15 October 2013

I am trying to find the family of an airman, Sgt Alan Jolly, who served with 148 Special Duties Squadron based in Brindisi Italy during the Second World War. His records show that he came from Fleetwood and returned there after his service ended.

His last known address was 12 The Strand, Rossall, Fleetwood, FY7 8NR. I am the daughter of Sgt John Rae, one of the airmen that Sgt Jolly served with. I would like to contact any family members regarding Sgt Jolly's RAF service.

I moved to the USA in 1980 and now live in California after having lived in Morecambe and Lytham St Annes.

ROSEMARY EDMEADS

California

This email was received on October 15th 2013 as I was sitting at Los Angeles International Airport for my flight to London Heathrow!!!

Dear Rosemary,

I am the son of Sgt Alan Jolly and have just read your article in the Fleetwood Gazette. I would love to hear from you and to learn more.

Yours Sincerely

Robert Alan Jolly.

CHAPTER 16

KRAKOW and BEYOND

On July 24, 2013 we began the long journey to Krakow. I woke up full of anticipation of the journey that I was about to embark upon. I had thought of this moment during the past months and now it was finally time to load the suitcases into the car and set off to Los Angeles International Airport. My next emotion was disappointment, when we were told there was a problem with the navigation computer. Our flight was rescheduled for the following day and we hastily made phone calls and set emails telling everyone of the delay. Everyone in Poland was sympathetic and we were told not to worry, plans for our arrival were hastily changed by our gracious hosts.

VISIT TO NIECEW and the KOSZYK FAMILY

Our day began early, both of us suffering from a twenty four hour flight delay and the long flight from Los Angeles, California.

One of Tomasz friends Zbignien Hajduk, collected us from the apartment and we set off on our journey to Niecew, but first stopping to meet Tomasz and Magda Jastrzębski's at their home in Wieliczka, which is famous for its Salt Mines. It was a meeting full of emotion because Tomasz and his family had spent the greater part of the past year writing and sending new information. He had become a true friend yet he was still someone I really did not know. I once heard someone say:

> "The reason we connect so easily and quickly with complete strangers is because the friendship is not of this life but the resumption of a friendship from another"

"I don't know if this is true but in this case it really does feel true" Their welcome was true and genuine and we were all very pleased to finally meet. Our language barrier was not apparent and with the help of Tomasz's sons and his good friend Zbignien (Ziggy) we somehow managed. Continuing on our way to Niecew, we made a visit to one of 500 cemeteries dotted around Krakow where the soldiers who fought in WW1 at Limowa are buried. These are memorials to the Eastern Front that is so often forgotten about in the rest of Europe. It is in a beautiful peaceful tranquil setting. Soldiers and officers of different armies buried side by side.

We reached Niecew after a two hour drive over twisty and bumpy roads and were greeted by the Koszyk family, Josef, his wife Helena and daughter Anka and later their son Andres who is home on holiday from Military School in Wroclan where he is training to be an Officer in the Polish Army. Adam Sikorski from Polish National Television and his crew were also there. In 2010 they had produced two programs about the crash of Halifax JP 162 and the excavation of the site, and were going to film this meeting which would continue that story. This visit was the continuing story of that event. To be greeted by a TV film crew took me by surprise but they were interested to finally meet a relative of one of the aircrew. Wreckage had been found several years before but they knew little about the airmen who flew the plane.

It is a story that has linked complete strangers together whose only real connection is that of Halifax JP 162. It was a journey I had looked forward to but today my emotions were very mixed. There was the feeling of excitement, sadness, and happiness all at once at meeting with the people who had been helping me. Josef Koyszk, the home owner, gave us a very warm welcome and told us about finding wreckage of the plane when he began the construction of his house. We were shown the site where JP162 had crashed into a small hillside.

**We finally meet! Edmeads and Koszyk families in Niecew,
Poland. Photo courtesy of Tomasz Jastrzbski**

It was quite a big crash site with cockpit and mid section of the
plane in Josef's yard and the tail end in the stream across the
road. The Koszyk family had lived in a house next to this land.
They had built this new house and Anka, Josef's daughter, told
me that growing up she had often found small pieces of
wreckage when she was playing in the yard.

As we stood in Josef's yard he said

"As a young boy I often listened to the story of the shooting
of Halifax. I did not know exactly where the plane fell. After
my wedding to Helena I moved to the village in which we
now live and in 1987 began working to build this house and
during land leveling the excavator discovered a part of the
plane. A lot of parts were lost because they were not
protected because at that time I did not have their own

buildings. I found a part of the engine, the fuel lines and molten aluminum."

The aileron on the Halifax had been used by the local villagers to dam up the stream which ran through the village of Niecew and other parts were used to build a footbridge. I am sure that these airmen would appreciate the ingenuity of these villagers in putting parts of their plane to such good use especially as the people of Poland were suffering great hardships.

Four of the crew had managed to parachute from the plane that night and survive. Their skipper had given to order "to bale out" The pilot, the upper and rear gunner did not survive. I can vaguely remember hearing the story about the events of that night. To know that so many years ago this was the "the small hillside" I had heard people talk about so many years ago. Now I was standing on the crash site talking with the people who were now living in the house they had built there. So many years had passed since that horrific event and now this is a peaceful, quiet place. Helena Koszyk who has lived in Niecew/ Wojnarowa area all her life told me the story that her parents remembered of the plane "falling from the sky" and now their daughter is living in the house on the spot where it fell. She can also remember as a child in school that the schoolchildren would place flowers on the "unknown soldier's grave" Now after all these years she is happy to know who those men are and meet me.

While Josef was telling us this story he showed us an old cooking pot that had a hole on the bottom that had been repaired by using a piece of aluminum from Halifax JP 162. A funny story which brought some laughter and lightness into what was in many ways a journey back to the sadness that the war had brought not just on me but also to the people of Poland. Josef kindly gave me two "fragments" of my dad's plane JP 162FS-S which I will take back to California. I was also introduced to Mr. Janusz Ostrega who presented me a book called "Partyzanci" by Stanislaw Derus. Mr. Ostraga also had connections to the Home Army as his father Strz. Bodo E Ostraga had been an AK soldier fighting to gain freedom for the Polish people. In this book were pictures of Sgt's Jolly and Peterson. There is an account of the crash with a list of the aircrew. The four airmen who survived were listed as members of:

Sklad osobowy 1 Batalionu 16pp AK "Barbara" w 1944

Sgt Robert Orlando Peterson RCAF.

F/O James Anderson RCAF

Sgt Alan Jolly RAFVR

Sgt Charlie Underwood RAFVR

The book is of course written in Polish but is a treasured memento of my visit.

In all the conversations we had throughout our visit Anka and Andres, Josef Koszyk's children acted as our interpreters as their father speaks no English and their mother Helena was able to understand some of what we said. We were taken to visit the village of Wojnarowa the place where the villagers of Niecew and Wojnarowa had buried the aircrew who did not survive. We met Mr. Jan Mika aged 85, who at the age of 12 saw all the events and plane crash of August 5, 1944. He retold the story of the night JP 162 crashed

"I was 13 years old when I noticed the night the accident aircraft. As it was the night I was not allowed to leave the house. In the morning I and a colleague went to the scene. I saw your dad lying head to the ground. I thought he was

Mr. Jan Miko, who witnessed JP162 crash, Tomasz Jastrzbski and author, Wojnarowa, Poland 2013. Photo courtesy of Anka Koszyk.

still alive but it was too late. We had to flee as German troops came. The German commander ordered to dig a grave in Wojnarowa because there was a Germany garrison stationed in the area."

He is a delightful man and although we had some difficulty communicating he had an interesting story to tell. I was able to place a plaque to commemorate the events that happened August 5th 1944 not just to remember Flt. Lt. James Girvan McCall, Sgt Clifford Aspinall and my dad Sgt John Frederick Cairney Rae who were killed but also remembering the brave villagers who gave these men a decent burial. I read a poem "Remember the Fallen" buy Analissa Range:

To Remember the Fallen

To remember the fallen
is not to remember how they fell
but to remember why and for what

To remember the fallen
is not only to remember their actions
but to remember the dream for which they fought

To remember the fallen
is not to remember how they fought
but to remember who they fought for

To remember the fallen
is to remember their reason
to remember their dreams
and to remember those they fought to save

To remember the fallen
we continue their fight
we carry their dreams
and we finish what they start.

I am not sure if the people who were listening understood what I was saying but reading it gave me a sense of peace that I had honored these men who had given their lives and who had lost so much. The people joined us were mainly family of Mr. Jan Mika and his neighbors. We were invited to come into the family home to enjoy a cool drink. This was much appreciated as we had been standing in the 95 degree heat. Mr Mika asked me for a picture of my dad which I was very pleased to give him.

We went to a hotel for a traditional Polish lunch which was hosted by the Koszyk family and then returned to their home where I shared information and pictures and answered their questions as best I could. Josef told me that he was really pleased to finally meet me as he had always wondered about the men on the airplane. One of his questions was "how did you find me?" That's another story for another day. My husband Robert and I were invited to visit the following weekend for a BBQ. We then drove back to Tomasz Jastrzębski home and met Magda his wife and sons Marik, Mateusz and his wife Beata and their daughter Viktoria. Plans were made for rest of week as we sat in their beautiful garden trying to keep cool. Arrangements were made for visits to various places such as the Salt Mine, The Home Army Museum and the Polish National Air Museum in Krakow. Just before we left Tomasz presented me with part of Halifax 162 FS-S, a memorable moment and something I will treasure.

A DAY OF REST

Krakow Square Lunch at a café in the beautiful Main Square. Hot Hot Hot!!!

We had arranged a meeting with Robert Reichert, now to be known a Robert the Younger or Young Robert to avoid confusion with my husband Robert to be known as Robert the Older!

Robert and Monika.

Robert Reichert, who I found by pure chance when I saw pictures he, had taken of Rakowicki Cemetery Allied Forces Section on All Saints Day November 1st. They were stunningly beautiful and very moving with all the graves lit with lanterns. It was the first time I realized that these brave men had never been forgotten by the people of Krakow. I took a chance and contacted Robert and it in many ways was the best thing I ever did. He is a wonderful young man who has been helping me during the past year. He has done this without being asked and I don't believe I would be meeting with all these wonderful people if he hadn't stepped in and helped me with my research. He came to visit us in the apartment on his way home from work and I was very pleased to meet him. He was concerned about us being tired after our long journey and was interested in my visit to Niecew. He has taken some time off work and will join us on our visit to the AK museum and The Polish National Air Museum.

MUSEUM DAY

Our friend Robert came to meet us and walk with us to the AK Home Army Museum where we were to meet with Tomasz and Marik. It was a pleasant walk as it was much cooler. We arrived and noticed that the Museum did not open until 11:00am. We were early! Suddenly three people came out from the museum and walked towards us and said "Welcome Rosemary we are pleased to meet you." What a surprise, we were to be their special guests and they had opened the museum especially for us. What an honour! We were shown around by our hosts Liliana Kaczor and Tadeusz Zaba, a Historian who described the artifacts and the history of the Armia Karjowa Home Army or also known as AK Army. We had been specially honored because the four airmen from JP 162 had marched with the AK Army during the time they had spent evading capture and their return home to England. The aircraft Historian group who helped in the excavation in 2010 is connected to this museum so when the wreckage of the aircraft had been discovered some had been displayed at the museum. I was able to present to our hosts with two plaques a 148 Squadron plaque and the other from the Royal Air Force Volunteer Reserve with which these seven airmen men had

Rakowicki Cemetery, Krakow, Poland.

served. We said farewell to our gracious hosts and thanked them for their kindness.

Our next stop was to be the Polish National Air Museum but on the way we made a small detour to visit Rakowicki Cemetery. Quite an emotional visit as I had last visited my dad in 1994 on the 50th Anniversary of my birth and his death. All of us stood quietly together and paid our respects to the crews who had flown on that ill fated mission on August 4/5 1944. These were the Blynn crew of JP 276 and Crabtree Crews of JP181 and of course the McCall crew. We also remembered the King crew in EB174 who had become POW's when their plane crashed. I made plans to visit this place again on August 4th the 69th. Anniversary.

We continued on to the Polish Air Museum where we were again special guests and were warmly welcomed by the curator and the staff. We sat and had a much welcomed cup of coffee or tea before we were shown around the museum by a young student Kamil Stasiak who is writing a dissertation for his university degree. The museum had an interesting collection of aircraft and a large collection of engines. This year the museum celebrates its 50th Birthday to be marked by special celebrations in September 2013. As we said good bye to our hosts and thanked them I marveled at everything that Tomasz had planned for our visit. It really made us feel very special. We were driven back to our comfortable apartment, "our home away from home" during our stay.

A VISIT TO WIELICZKA SALT MINES

Marik Jastrzębski came to the apartment to take us to the Salt Mines in Wieliczka his home town. He had traveled in by bus but we decided to take a taxi for the return journey.

My husband Robert and cousin Shelagh went on the tour to the oldest Salt Mine in the world; again they were special guests and were taken to join the tour without having to wait in the hot sun. Tomasz seems to have special connections everywhere we go!!!! I was able to sit with Magda and Tomasz and exchange all the information we had collected about the crew of Halifax JP 162. We managed to do this without the help of our interpreters (their sons) by using a dictionary, Google translate and sign language and the occasional comment by Tomasz "one moment", we laughed but felt no awkwardness at our total lack of language skill especially me with my non existent Polish.

Tomasz gave me a collection of letters and correspondence between a Mr. Jacek Popiel who at the age of 16 was part of the AK Army and knew Sgt Charlie Underwood and Sgt Alan Jolly. It was planned that Mr. Popiel would be at Josef Koszyk's home to talk with me but sadly he was in the hospital. I think he would have been a very interesting person to talk with. Charlie Underwood and Alan Jolly had served with Jacek Popiel in the Battalion Barbara. It was an unexpected surprise that I was given this information plus the fact that I now have photographs six out of the seven aircrew. The only missing airman is Fl/Officer PJ Anderson. More pieces of the puzzle still to be solved. When we finally arrived home in California there was a surprise when I did open the files on the disc I had been given. There was a photo of Flt. Sgt. Anderson. My crew pictures were now complete.

The family arrived and we all sat down to a wonderful meal which Magda had prepared for us. We watched the wedding video of Mateusz and Beata.

Tomasz, Magda, Beata and Viktoria at their home in Wieliezka Poland 2013.

In the afternoon we sat in the garden and enjoyed an afternoon of wonderful conversation even with the language barrier (boy is Polish a hard language). I gave the family their gifts which everyone seemed to appreciate. Plans were made for our visits to the Kazimirz (Jewish section of Krakow) and Wawel Castle and the new Underground Museum in the main square. A friend of Tomasz's, Marchin, who we had met at the Polish National Air Museum offered to drive us back to the apartment. After a short rest we went for a walk around the main square and stopped at a café for a drink.

DISCOVERING KRAKOW

Today we are tourists in Krakow. It is another very hot day and hopefully our walk in Krakow can be done using the shady part of the streets or as the Polish call it "the shadows". Our first stop is the new "Underground Museum". In 2005 the Main Square in Krakow around the Cloth Hall was excavated. This was a great undertaking and has resulted in many antiquities being discovered and resulting in this museum under the Cloth Hall. It is a fascinating place to visit and shows all the early development of Krakow back to times before the Middle Ages.

Our next stop was what we thought to be a jewelry shop specializing in the much sought after amber. It was in fact a museum. I thought some of the pieces looked extremely heavy because of their size but in fact when Magda asked the curator to show me two large pieces I was surprised how light they were. There were some beautiful pieces. From there we walked slowly through the streets towards Warwel Castle and decided on a visit to the cathedral and walk around the courtyards would be enough energy spent on such a hot day. The views from the terraces and ramparts gave a wonderful sight of the old and new Krakow. We walked down to the promenade by the Vistula River and saw the Krakow Dragon.

Slowly walking to the Kazimierz district we saw the Old Tram Museum and the remains of the Old Jewish Ghetto. The tall deserted buildings had been left so suddenly by their owners after they had been rounded up and sent to the camps made this a hauntingly sad place. We stopped at a café to have a cold drink and say our goodbyes to Tomasz, Magda and Marik who were setting off on Sunday for their holiday to the Baltic Coast. A sad farewell because they had made us feel so welcome and part of their family. I told Tomasz that this was not "Goodbye" just "see you soon" but never the less I still felt very sad that our time together had passed so quickly.

Today shortly after we left Tomasz and his family we heard a haunting sound, a siren. The whole of Poland stood for a minute in total silence to remember and honor the memory of thousands of people who gave their lives on that day for their precious beloved city of Warsaw from the hated enemy! This was August 1st the first day of the Warsaw Uprising which was to last 63 days. On the fifth day of the Uprising my dad Sgt John Rae and sixteen other airmen from the Royal Air Force 148 Special Duties Squadron gave their lives after successfully dropping much needed supplies to the Home Army. How could I ever forget the Warsaw Uprising?

Tomasz wrote to me

> "Every year on August 1 this moment just shakes me. We also stood paying tribute to the men like your father. The Big thanks to all!
>
> Sending you two links showing the event
>
> We greet you warmly
>
> Tom and Magda'

BACK TO NIECEW

Josef Koszyk arrived at our apartment to drive is to his home in Niecew where we were to spend the weekend with his family. Boy is he a fast driver!! The trip which had taken us over two hours the previous week took us only one hour and a half. We went by a different route through Nowy Sacz and along the road by the lake it was a good smooth road. Josef speaks no English and we don't speak Polish. What to do? Converse in German of course! Josef had worked in Germany for many years and was quite fluent and my husband Robert had last spoken German over thirty years ago. No problem somehow they managed to communicate.

We were greeted by Helena his wife and Anka their daughter and of course the usual ice cream and cake. This is the way Polish families greet guests in their home. Later we had a meal which was similar to an afternoon tea with cold meats cheese and salads. We were to stay in a hotel in the next town as they thought we would be more comfortable so later Anka and Andres drove us there.

They collected us the next morning and Anka prepared breakfast. Quite confusion when I asked for jam and she brought ham!!! There was much laughter!

On Saturday we drove to a small spa town called Krynica in the Tetra Mountains. Everywhere the summer flowers were in full bloom in the gardens, on balconies and hanging flower baskets. We drove through some beautiful countryside and rode the cable cars to the top. Helena had bought some local fudge and we sampled it on our ride up. Delicious!! It was peaceful sitting at the top and we strolled taking in the views and taking lots of pictures of the flowers and stopped for a cold drink. On our ride down in the cable car Robert my husband gave Anka instructions that he would get out first I would go next and Anka was to give me a push if I wasn't fast enough because the cable car did not stop. Anka thought this was very funny.

Our next stop was to walk through the town to visit the spa and taste the waters which we assured by everyone would keep us healthy. This reminded me of Cheltenhan in the Cotswold's where we had lived, which became famous for its spa and miracle waters. The gardens as always were full of color despite the heat.

The evening was spent preparing for the BBQ in the new gazebo. Josef has his own building company and the gazebo had had since our last visit had a thatched roof installed. I have never seen so much meat for just for the six of us but it was great fun and I am sure Josef and Robert had sore heads by the end of the evening!! We were driven back to our hotel (Josef had been the builder) where there was a large wedding reception being held so not much sleep that night.

Once again we were collected and served breakfast. We stopped at the grave site in Wojnarowa and I laid crosses from the Royal British Legion for the three airmen on the 69th Anniversary of the loss of Halifax JP 162FS-S August 4/5 1944. We made our farewells to Helena and Andrew and Josef and Anka drove us back to Krakow "at warp speed" It was a wonderful weekend and I was sad to say goodbye to such kind and generous people.

REMEMBERANCE SUNDAY

We arrived back in Krakow and later I braved the heat and walked to the Main Square to buy flowers from the market stall for out trip to the cemetery later that afternoon when we hoped it would be cooler. Afterward we had lunch at Halvelka in the

"Not Forgotten" Author visiting the grave of her father Sgt. John Rae in Krakow Aug 4, 2013. Photo courtesy of Robert Reichert, Krakow.

main square. This has become our favorite place to eat. We took a taxi and were met by Robert and Monika and we walked to the Allied section together only to find the gate shut tight. With a little bit of ingenuity we got in and placed the flowers on the graves of my dad John Rae, James McCall and Clifford Aspinall. We also remembered the aircrew from the Blynn and Crabtree planes. This was the 69th Anniversary of that ill fated mission on August 4/5th 1944 when the crews were told not to fly to Warsaw as it was too dangerous and were given orders to fly to "safe drop zones" What irony, the Polish pilots disobeyed orders and flew to aid their fellow countrymen in Warsaw and survived whereas the RAF planes obeyed and lost the majority of their planes. My friends Robert and Monika placed flowers and lanterns on the three graves and Robert made the comment that he now felt he knew these men and they were no longer just names on a stone. He has been a wonderful support and I am honored to call him a "true friend" I signed the book kept in the box at the cemetery. Rakowicki Cemetery is a fascinating place to visit and we made our way to the older part of the cemetery so I could place some flowers on Robert's family grave especially for his grandfather an Officer on the Polish Army who had been rounded up and taken away by the Russians never to be heard of again!! Quite a trek but we passed some interesting grave sites. We said our goodbyes and we walked back to the apartment.

TOURISTS

A quiet day to reflect and rest and to be tourists once again!

We ventured into the Cloth Hall which stands in the center of the main Square in Krakow and now holds a huge assortment of stalls selling mementos of Poland and lots of Amber. A shopping expedition what fun!!

Robert my husband went off exploring the city and came back to take us to lunch at the Franchusca Hotel where we had stayed on our previous visit to Krakow in 1994. The hotel had been built in the 1920's and it is full of old world charm. It was a wonderful setting and great service for our "Expresso Lunch" A three course lunch for 20 zlotys (about $6) a head.

Throughout our visit to Poland we were struck by the beauty of the countryside the rolling green hills and the beautiful snow capped mountains in the distance. We were so fortunate to be able to enjoy much of this beauty and enjoy sharing the day to day living of our friends. We had paid a visit to a small village which was the oldest inhabited village of wooden houses. They were quite stunning and beautifully maintained and cared for by their owners, just being able to wonder around on our own enjoying strolling down the main street taking our time taking lots of pictures. There were many villagers busy working tending their gardens which were in full bloom. In all the places we have visited the beautiful flowers in window boxes, in planters and in the gardens have been just wonderful. After all the hard winters that the Polish people endure I am sure they must look forward to being able to see such an abundance of color.

We visited Zacopane in the Tatra Mountains and as we strolled the busy streets we tried to avoid the crowds. It was not at all like the place we had visited with Koszyk family a few days earlier. Life seemed to be at a much slower pace in the many small villages and everywhere we drove by the rivers there were always lots of people enjoying the cooler air of the riverside. There we always interesting old churches to visit many of them made of wood and beautiful views of the mountains and valley's.

Our evenings in Krakow always provided us with an interesting array of sights to see and enjoy. There always seemed to be a festival in one of the many squares and we would spend the evening walking to a nearby square which seemed to have variety different festivals during our stay. No sooner than one festival was over than another was being set up. We enjoyed a peroggi festival sampling the many different types of peroggi savory and sweet and then strolled through the main square which seemed to come alive as families came out to stroll in the cooler evening air when the sun went down. We would finally find a seat in one of the many restaurants which surrounded the square enjoying a meal or a drink and just watch the beautiful horse drawn carriages drive slowly by or the children playing with lighted toys which they shot up in the sky.

SCHINDLER FACTORY, KRAKOW.

Today I was to meet Agnieszka Partridge who is a TV Journalist in Krakow and writer married to Kristopher an engineer who

works for the BBC in London. We arrived at the Oscar Schindler
Factory where Agnies was there to meet us and take us on a
tour. It is a well laid out exhibit of how Schindler was able to
employ some of the Jewish people from the Camps where they
were held by the Germans.

After the tour Agnieszka and I sat down to discuss my research
and to share information. She was at that moment writing a
book about the village of Plesna near Tarnow and has decided
to add a chapter about Halifax JP 162FS-S because of the fact
that the four crew who were able to "bale out." Anderson,
Peterson, Jolly and Underwood had been hidden in safe houses
in the area and her grandmother had known of these men.

Agnieszka told me the story of Salomea Gaciarz known as
"Jodelka" her grandmother, who was a member 16 Infantry
Regiment "Barbara" a partisan section of the AK Army. Her
grandfather Stanislaw Gaciarz "Ferbal" also served in the AK
Army. Many years ago, in the late 1980's her grandmother had
shown Agnieszka a photograph of four men two of which
were "British Pilots" (this was the name that Polish people
called all airmen). On the back of the photo Agnies said the
name of Sgt. Charles Underwood, was written. The man who
was responsible for the safety of two airmen was Wladyslaw
Zatorski nickname "Lado" who was the adjutant of Eugeniusz
Borowski "Leliwa" the commander of the battalion was also
in the picture. He was murdered on September 1, 1945 by the
Communist Security Office. He was in hiding because he was a
partisan and did not want to accept the Soviet Influence after
the Liberation. The other man in the picture was an unknown
Jew who was also in hiding.

The photo was believed to have been taken in January 1945 by a
photographer in Tarnow after the Russians had entered Tarnow
and the men were about to make the long journey back to
England. They had been staying in a house whose owner

George Poetschke, 9 Kollataja, Tarnow was also hiding a Jewish girl. According to Charles Underwood, the owner had a friend who was a "cover" and in that same house German Officers were entertained. The men told the partisans they were airmen from a plane which had been shot down near Wojnarowa August 5th. Agnieszka had always wondered why the airmen were always seen in their uniform and I said I thought that if they had been caught out of uniform they could have been shot as spies. She eventually traced Sgt Underwood to his home in Nottingham and was able to meet with him and record his story. She showed him the picture but he said he was not on the picture it was indeed Sgt Robert Peterson from Canada and the other airman was Sgt Alan Jolly from Fleetwood.

I had spoken to Agnieszka before I left for Krakow when she and her husband Kris had contacted me after reading my story on a group site Operations Dark of the Moon of which I was a member. She had also been searching again for Sgt. Underwood as was I. We exchanged the information I had and began to realize the story had I been told which had seemed so far fetched, matched exactly with hers. I had also recently been given information from Tomasz Jastrzebski which included letters Charlie Underwood had written to a Jacek Popiel whom he had met while serving with the Home Army and all three stories matched. We were now finally meeting face to face and I was able to provide her with additional photos which she appreciated and I shared with her my long journey to reach this point of my visit to Krakow. She shared her rough draft of her book and showed me the quote I have often used "as long as their names are spoken among the people they will never be forgotten." This is a quote my friend Terry Marker shared with me when I first joined the group (Operations Dark of the Moon) which he had founded and it is one I have never forgotten. It has a special meaning for me and it keeps me going as I try to keep the memory of the men who flew JP162 alive. Agnieszka plans to quote it in her chapter about this airplane.

It was a wonderful meeting and this again has helped me in this long journey I have undertaken.

Robert Reichert & author

LAST DAY

We met with Robert at the wonderful Margo Café. He had collected the necessary, documents in order I could take the "fragments" I had been given by Tomasz and Josef of Halifax JP162FS-S back to California. Apparently it is illegal to remove any artifacts from Poland. It seemed quite a complicated procedure but it was done efficiently and all was in order. I now believe that these documents have given these fragments provenance and added to the story of this plane. As we sat and talked Robert gave me a book on the Warsaw Uprising, a calendar of Krakow and a USB stick with all the beautiful photos he had taken of our visit. He had to return to work and I was very sad to say goodbye to him. He is a very special caring person with a wonderful sense of humor and incredible kindness. I was overwhelmed by his one simple act of kindness last year when he visited my dad's grave in Rakowicki last November 1st 2012. He took pictures and posted a beautiful tribute. His interest in my struggle to find more about my dad these airmen has made me even more determined to keep going with this search. He has become a true friend and one I miss already.

My Robert had been determined to eat at a "Milk Bar", introduced during the Russian occupation it was a cheap place to eat. I wasn't really impressed as our Espresso Lunch at the Franchuska Hotel with all its ambiance was a far better deal.

We later went for drinks and a coffee at Halvalka our favorite restaurant in the Main Square. It had rained heavily earlier in the day. The streets were wet, and glistened in the night light, as were the chairs but who cares when you are sitting in the midst of one of the oldest and most beautiful town squares in the world. All through our last night the sky was lit with lightening and the thunder rumbled. I wonder if the crew of Halifax JP 162 was trying to tell us something. Maybe just simply to say "thank you for not forgetting us."

My journey has come to an end and I am sad to leave. Krakow is a beautiful city with welcoming, kind and friendly people. It is a city that seems to keep beckoning me back and it seems that I have been cast under its spell. It is a special place and one that holds a very special meaning for me. During the past two weeks I have been met with nothing but kindness by the families who I got to know through emails sent to Robert in Krakow to be translated, returned to me in California and then sent back to Poland over this past year. A strange way to get to know someone so far away but for us it worked.

We have become friends and have a special connection through the airmen on that ill fated mission 69 years ago August 4/5/1944 who were on the last flight of:

Halifax JP 162FS

"S for sugar...Still on Sortie, August 4th/5th, 1944.

Flt Lt, James Girvan McCall RAFVR 23,
Pilot from Edinburgh, Scotland.

F/O James Phillip Anderson RCAF 35,
Navigator from Toronto, Canada.

Flt. Sgt. Robert Orlando Peterson RCAF 30,
Bomb Aimer, Revelstoke, B.C., Canada.

Sgt, Charles Underwood RAFVR 20,
Flt. Engineer from Nottingham, England.

Sgt. Alan Jolly RAFVR, 22, Wireless Operator/
Air Gunner from Fleetwood, England.

Sgt Clifford Aspinall RAFVR 37,
Upper Turret Gunner from Blackpool, England.

Sgt John Frederick Cairney Rae RAFVR 33,
Rear Gunner from Dalmuir, Scotland.

CHAPTER 17

THE FINDING OF JP162 WRECKAGE

Exploration Group PTH New Market was formed in 2006. This exploration group is connected to the Home Army Museum in Krakow. Its members are all interested in recent military history of WW1 and WW II for the years 1917 to 1945. They are particularly interested in Military Aviation History. During the time that this group has been formed they had found and carried out several excavations of aircraft and shared their findings.

Koszyk family home stands on the crash site of Halifax JP162. Photo courtesy of Tomasz Jastrzbski.

The group of aircraft historians became interested in searching for an aircraft that had been supplying the Polish underground which had crashed in August 1944. A few years earlier the wreckage of another aircraft Halifax JP 276A flying on this same mission had been located and an excavation on a much larger scale was undertaken funded by the Warsaw Uprising Museum in Warsaw. This aircraft was Halifax JP276 that of Flt. Lt. Arnold Blynn, RCAF and his crew who were all killed.

A family now lived in a house built on the crash site of the aircraft that the group was interested in. This was Halifax JP 162FS of RAF 148 Squadron which had crashed in the hillside in the village of Niecew on its return flight to the base in Brindisi, Italy after dispatching is load to partisans near Miechow. The homeowner gave his permission for the excavation by the exploration group to go ahead

This excavation was on a much smaller scale than that of Halifax JP 276A but it never the less established the correct location of the aircraft and several parts of the plane were discovered. They carried out this excavation in two stages during the winter of 2009 and again in the spring of 2010. They found the biggest pieces of the aircraft structure on a memorable Sunday April 10, 2010.

Several pieces of the wreckage were transported to the Home Army Museum in Krakow and a display was set up by the museum.

The team learned much from this excavation. How the burning plane had crashed into the hillside and killed the pilot Flt.Lt. McCall, Sgt Aspinall; and Sgt Rae. The other airmen jumped from the plane and were helped by the Battalion "Barbara 16ppAK Army and hidden from the Germans by the local villagers.

Wreckage of Halifax JP162 found during excavation winter 2010 Photo courtesy of Tomasz Jastrzbski

A record of this excavation was made by Polish National TV station being present and recording the progress. Later this was made into a short TV documentary shown on Polish Television in 2010.

The members of this Aircraft Historians gathered together all their information to make a report. They knew little of the airmen who flew in this plane but they were always grateful to them for the aid they brought to Poland so many years ago.

During one of the groups meetings in 2013 they decided that they would apply to the Polish Government to get recognition for the crew of JP162. They felt that this crew should receive a special honour for their bravery in supplying the AK Home Army. Paperwork was submitted and a copy of their application was sent to the author by Robert Springwald.

Fast forward to August 2013. Some of the members of this group and the home owner welcomed the daughter of one of the airmen. She was the daughter of Sgt, John Cairney Rae who had been the rear gunner on the Halifax. This visit was recorded by Polish National Television and edited together with the previous program and shown once more on Polish National Television in September 2013. From this small undertaking by this group much had transpired and they found great satisfaction that their effort had born fruit.

CHAPTER 18

SOME FINAL THOUGHTS

Many of the people I met whilst I was visiting Krakow seem to think that there should be a permanent memorial to the crew of JP 162. In many of the other communities where other aircraft belonging to the Allied Forces were lost on that same mission or on other missions the local communities have erected a memorial to the crews of those airplanes. After visiting the home and beautiful gardens of Josef and Helena Koszyk in Niecew I begin to wonder if this is necessary. They of course wanted to show great respect for these men who helped Poland when help was so badly needed. It is hard to believe that this was the site of such a horrific scene so many years ago when the people of Poland were suffering such hardships and the airmen from this airplane were simply trying to help. The house that Josef Koszyk built, on this site, for his family in Niecew is in a quiet peaceful community in the Polish countryside with beautifully tended gardens. Perhaps a small plaque is all that is required. These kind people showed how much they care by the kindness that was shown to me during my visit.

The tragic event of the crash of Halifax JP162, with the loss of three of the crew and four brave airmen who survived (with the protection of the partisans and the AK with whom they fought) has, so many years later brought together complete strangers in thanksgiving and remembrance. All of us have a special connection through this aircraft. It is one I did not expect and I am sure that Josef, Tomasz and Robert will agree, out of the horrors and tragedies of an ill fated mission, out of sadness and despair has come something very special.

To me this journey has brought peace and the knowledge that these brave airmen are still thought of so highly by the Polish people and are cared for by so many. To three special people Robert, Tomasz and Josef the names written on three headstones in Rakowicki Cemetery in the Allied Forces section are no longer just three more names. They now feel a special pride that they know these men. These men have spent countless hours researching after the wreckage of JP 162 was discovered and now they know the men who flew in this plane all those years ago.

We were not the only family who lost a loved one who served in the Royal Air Force Volunteer Reserve. Many families share our sadness and loss. Over 125,000 Royal Air Force Volunteer Reserve airmen, all volunteers, served their country in a time of need, 55,573 of them never came home!

I thought of my dad as I often do these days, during this long journey. What questions would I like to ask him after all these years? Maybe if it were possible to spend a day with him, to hear his voice, to see him smile and laugh and to tell him how proud I am of him. But to also tell how I wish he had not gone away and not returned but instead had come back and been there to watch me grow. I hope that he to would be proud.

I did not realize that this story would become such a big part of my life and I do not think my family quite understood fully how important it was for me to make this journey. Maybe it is a good thing that I have been able to make the long journey to Krakow, to meet with the people who also have connections to my dad and to finally see the place I had so often heard about "the hillside" where his plane crashed or see his name etched on his headstone in the cemetery in Krakow. I believe it has helped me gain the peace that I have been seeking for so long without realizing. I hope by writing about these events they will now understand. I have told this story with complete openness and maybe in a way which has made me vulnerable to criticism by those who may not know me as well but that is a risk I was willing to take when I started this journey. Life cannot always be written in the way we would like and given time it would be nice to go back and write it better. That certainly would be the easy way out but it is what we have experienced through living our lives whether it be good or bad and it cannot simply be brushed aside or easily separated. If we leave out the bad we also loose some of the good which has been intertwined. Our past comes as a package deal and we cannot tell some of the story without telling it all.

I think it is time for me to close my files and step back and acknowledge that whatever may happen to this story, I have told it in a way that I hope people will understand. Even though I did not know my father John Rae I have finally come to know a man who I can be really proud. Knowing that in such a time he was ready to loose everything, a young wife and a daughter he hardly knew. A daughter who loved him then and still does today.

I am sure that this story of Halifax JP 162FS-S will continue. This story will always have loose ends and as much as I would like to tie up all the loose ends that may not be possible so it may fall to someone else to continue this story as other information is uncovered. These brave men can never be forgotten.

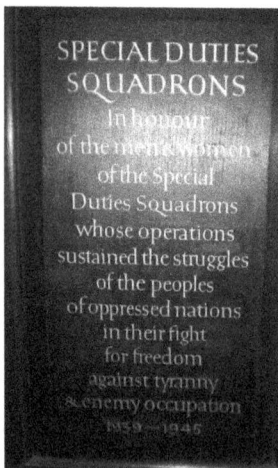

SPECIAL DUTIES SQUADRONS

In honour of the men & women of the Special Duties Squadrons whose operations sustained the struggles of the peoples of oppressed nations in their fight for freedom against tyranny & enemy occupation 1939–1945

Memorial for Special Duties Squadrons dedicated at St Clement Danes Church, London. October 18 2013.

172

Just as I felt that this long journey had come to a close something else very special but unexpected occurred. On October 18, 2013 a Special Service of Thanksgiving and Dedication of a Memorial to "Special Duties Squadrons" was held at the Royal Air Force Church St Clement Danes in London. Once again I set off on another long journey.

The church is beautiful in its simplicity. During WW2 it had been heavily bombed but its reconstruction with plain simple windows and the beautiful tiled floor, each tile representing a Royal Air Force Squadron is stunning. The pews are simple some with the names of important officers in the RAF. Ironically one of the pews is named after Sir John Slesser who had ordered the aircrew flying on the night of August 4/5 1944 not to fly to Warsaw!

This service was organized by the Royal Air Force Benevolent Fund and Special Forces Club. There has been much controversy about the airmen who were attached to Bomber Command but in fact these airmen from Special Duties Squadrons were flying vastly different but equally dangerous missions. I believe that because their missions were classed as "SECRET" they have not being recognized either at the Bomber Command Memorial or by being awarded the Bomber Command Clasp for their service and ultimate sacrifice.

Those of us who attended put all that aside and took part in a very simple but moving service. A simple memorial was dedicated to the airmen from all the squadrons who had become part of Special Duties Squadrons flying these long and dangerous missions. The service was attended by several veterans of the squadron along with family members and friends of these airmen and of course the young airmen and officers of the present day Royal Air Force. I was very proud to be able to attend and to meet with several people who had become friends through "Operations Dark of the Moon" who are all connected in some way to the airmen who served in RAF 148 Squadron. After the service a small reception was held in Australia House. In many ways the service served as a reminder that we cannot forget that so many lives were lost and in many cases the airmen had been forgotten. To me this was the end of a year where I had made so many discoveries, traveling many thousands of miles to do so, but it seemed the perfect ending.

As long as I am able to do so I will continue to speak the name of my dad Sgt. John Frederick Cairney Rae and those names of the men he served with in 148 Special Duties Squadron and by doing so they will never be forgotten.

REMEMBERING THE CREW OF HALIFAX JP 162

By Rosemary Edmeads

Skipper McCall was proud of his crew
those airmen who flew with him on JP162
Anderson, Peterson and Underwood too
Rae and Aspinall and Jolly
these were the men that he knew?

They flew long missions for Special Ops
Working together to deliver supplies
To the Polish partisans and our other allies

The flights from Brindisi were long and so cold
my dad, the rear gunner, sat cold and alone
in his own little turret, protecting his crew
from the dangers that lurked in the skies that they flew.

They worked well together, each man did his task
Navigating and flying their huge aircraft alone in the sky
to their drop zones and back to their base once again.

They flew with each other night after night
dropping supplies so the Home Armies could fight
So that their Homeland of Poland should once more be free.

On August the fourth nineteen forty four
they set off again to aide beleaguered Warsaw
in what was to become a more difficult mission
a disastrous night for the squadron we learn
that the men and their airplanes would never return.

The losses were heavy their luck had run out
But they aided the Poles of that there's no doubt
What a terrible way to describe their demise
These men who had risked and flown those skies
To deliver much needed supplies
To help other people whose need was so great?

These men were the crew of an airplane I knew
that was Halifax JP 162
my father was one of its special crew
who have not been forgotten by the people they helped
nor by the children that two never knew

They're still loved and remembered these seventy long years
since that long ago night when they flew. Before all the tears.
When so many men in so many crews
would never return to the ones that they loved
they are buried together in a land far away.

So remember the McCall aircrew of JP 162
seven brave airmen we mustn't forget
because we own them an enormous debt
three of these airmen never came home
and four of the others fought long and so hard
to return to their homeland and the families they loved.

My journey has been long and continues today
My story is told and I am so proud to say,
I will never forget the pride that I feel
Remembering those airmen who gave of their all.
Who were part of the crew simply known as McCall
As long as we mention their names as we speak
we will never forget these brave men who flew
their last mission in Halifax JP 162.

CHAPTER 19

"LEST WE FORGET"

This year, 2014, marks the 70th Anniversary of the tragic events which occurred in August 1944. The Warsaw Uprising began and the loss of so many Allied Aircrew who flew these dangerous missions to help the heroic partisan fighters in the beleaguered city of Warsaw, none more so than the tragic events which occurred on 4/5 August 1944 when RAF 148 Squadron lost so many fine airmen.[40]

Their names are recorded here as a permanent reminder of their sacrifice.

RAF 148 Special Duties Squadron Losses 4/5 August, 1944 aiding the Polish AK Army during the Warsaw Uprising:

Aircraft and names of the airmen were taken from the Operations Record Book of the Squadron--so many tragic entries, poignant in its briefness. These records are for one single night 4/5 August, 1944.

Halifax LW 294 (Snow Crew) Time Up 19:58 Down 21:25. Returned early. Task was abandoned when it was found out that the guns would not fire. On landing a tire burst, aircraft caught fire and was totally destroyed.

Halifax JP 223 (French Crew) Time Up 20:02 Down 05:03. Operation successful. Light flack. 6 packages dropped.

Halifax JP295 (Brown Crew) Time up 19:57 Down 04:49. No reception at primary target or secondary target.

Halifax JP 181 (Crabtree Crew) Time up 19:57 Down------ Nothing further heard from this aircraft. It is presumed lost.

Halifax JP276 (Blynn Crew) Time up: 19:56------no news was received from this aircraft after take off. It is presumed lost.

Halifax JP162 (McCall Crew) Time up: 19:59------Reached drop zone and made a successful drop. This aircraft failed to return to base. Nothing further heard. It is presumed lost.

Halifax EB 147 (King Crew) Time up: 20:22 Down------Nothing further heard Presumed lost.

All the aircraft departed from Campo Casale, Brindisi, Italy with supplies for the Polish Home Army fighting on the streets of Warsaw.

The names of airmen on the Squadron Losses List of 4/5 August, 1944:

Aircraft: Halifax JP276-A, "A-ABLE"

Flt. Lt. Arnold Raymond Blynn, RCAF Pilot
Sgt. Frederick George Wenham, RAFVR Flight Engineer
P/O. George Alfred Chapman, RCAF Navigator
F/Sgt. Charles Burton Wylie, RCAF Air Bomber
F/O. Harold Leonard Brown, RCAF Wireless Op/Air Gunner
F/Sgt. Arthur George William Liddell, RCAF Air Gunner
Sgt. Kenneth James Ashmore, RAFVR Air Gunner
All buried at Krakow Rakowicki Cemetery, Poland.

Aircraft: Halifax JP181-X FS-X "X-X-RAY

P/O. Charles William Crabtree, RAFVR Pilot
Sgt. Dennis Aird, RAFVR Flight Engineer
F/Sgt. Dennis John Mason, RAFVR Navigator
F/Sgt. Alexander Bennett, RAAF Air Bomber
W/O. John Aloysius Carroll RAFVR Wireless Op.
F/Sgt. Charles Alec Beanland, RCAF Air Gunner
Sgt. Alexander Sandilands, RAFVR Air Gunner
All buried at Krakow Rakowicki Cemetery, Poland.

Aircraft: Halifax JP162-S, FS-S "S-SUGAR"

Flt.Lt. James Girvan McCall, RAFVR Pilot
Sgt. Clifford Aspinall, RAFVR Air Gunner
Sgt. John Frederick Cairney Rae, RAFVR Air Gunner
All buried at Rakowicki Cemetery Poland
F/O. Phillip James Anderson, RCAF Navigator*
F/Sgt Robert Orlando Peterson, RCAF Bomb Aimer*
Sgt. Alan Jolly RAFVR, Wireless Op. /Air Gunner*
Sgt Charles Underwood, RAFVR Flight Engineer*
*Parachuted from plane and were aided by Polish AK partisans.

Aircraft: Halifax EB 147-K FS-K

F/O L.J.G. King, RAFVR Pilot
F/O. O.J. Watson, RAFVR Air Bomber
F/O J.W. Symington, RAFVR Navigator
Sgt J. Stewart RAFVR Wireless/Op.
Sgt. T.O. Hammond, RAFVR Flight Engineer
Sgt. R.C. Greenfell, RAFVR Air Gunner
W/O. S.A. Miller, RAFVR Dispatcher

All crew survived, 6 were taken POW. F/O. Symington evaded capture and was looked after by AK partisans.

The Names of airmen who returned 4/5 August, 1944.

Aircraft: Halifax LW 294-Z

Sgt. F.N. Snow, RAFVR Pilot
F/O. T. Dovey, RAFVR
F/Sgt. BW Ellison, RAFVR
Sgt. C.W. Robinson, RAFVR
Sgt C.H. King. RAFVR
F/Sgt. F. White, RAAF
Sgt. S.M. Johnson, RAFVR

Aircraft: Halifax: JP223-W

W/O S.R. French, RCAF Pilot
F/Sgt. R.K. Marsan, RCAF
F/O. W.D. Hopkinson, RCAF
F/Sgt. H. Lomas, RAFVR
Sgt. W. Hawkins, RAFVR
Sgt. J. Candy, RAFVR
Sgt. R.N. Blake, RAFVR

Aircraft: JP 295-P

W/O. D. Brown, RAFVR Pilot
F/Lt. R. D. Moore, RAFVR
F/Lt. L. Barrett, RCAF
F/Lt. C.C. Isaac, RAFVR
F/Sgt. J.L. Clark, RAFVR
W/O.T.B. Brown, RAFVR
W/O. H. Smith, RCAF
F/Sgt Moulder, RAFVR Extra crewman

APPENDECIS

Appendix A

ROYAL AIR FORCE ACRONYMS

The Royal Air Force used Acronyms to abbreviate long titles. This method was used to make reporting on service records shorter and easier to read once you learned them.

3RC	Padgate Recruiting Center.
ACRC	Air Crew Recruiting Center
ACSB	Air Crew Selection Board
AGS	Air Gunners School
BAF	Balkan Air Force
CMAF	Central Mediterranean Air Force
Flt. Eng.	Flight Engineer
Flt. Lt.	Flight Lieutenant
Flt. Sgt.	Flight Sergeant
FTR	Failed to Return
FU	Ferry Unit
HCU	Heavy Conversion Unit
ITU	Initial Training Center
LAPG	London Aircraft Production Group
MI	Military Intelligence
MI9	Escape and Evasion
OACU	Overseas Aircrew Conversion Unit
OADU	Overseas Aircraft Delivery Unit
OSUP	Overseas Aircraft Preparation Unit
OTU	Operational Training Unit
PAF	Polish Air Force
P/O.	Pilot Officer
RAAF	Royal Australian Air Force

RAF	Royal Air Force
RAFVR	Royal Air Force Volunteer Reserve
RC	Recruiting Center No placed before letters indicate town/city
RCAF	Royal Canadian Air Force
SAAF	South African Air Force
Sgt.	Sergeant
SOE	Special Operations Executive
W/O.	Warrant Officer
W/Op	Wireless Operator

Appendix B

This appendix consists of copies of letters and signals with regards to the events which occurred on August 4/5 1944:

Transcript of message sent August 6, 1944 from Headquarters Mediterranean Allied Air Forces to 148 Special Duties Squadron.

From: Air Marshal Sir John Slessor, K.C.B, D.S.C. M.C.
Headquarters
Mediterranean Allied Air Force

JCS.14   TOP SECRET and PERSONAL   6 August 1944

To: 148 Squadron, B.A.F.
From M.A.A.F
6th August 1944.

"Dear Pitt,

I am sorry to hear about your losses in Poland the night before last. I feel I must write and congratulate you on the magnificent work your Squadron has been doing recently. I am afraid you have been very hard worked, but I can only assure you that it has been of greatest value and I hope you will let all your chaps know how grateful I am for the splendid work they have done.

The staff is getting busy about your crew position. I am afraid you are in rather a bad way at the moment. I gather it was partly due to a lot of crews coming up tour expired at the same moment and I am sure you can keep an eye on the stagger of crews. There was also a mix up about the Sterling re-equipment programme; but S.P.S.O tells me that he is doing what he can and hopes to improve your position shortly".

Yours sincerely,

J. Slessor

Wing Commander D.L.Pitt, D.F.C. A.F.C.
Officer Commanding,
No 148 Squadron
Royal Air Force
Central Mediterranean Forces

This was the letter sent to the Commanding Officer of 148 Special Duties Squadron after the disastrous mission an August 4/5th 1944 from Air Marshall Slessor at Headquarters of Mediterranean Forces.

The following is a congratulatory signal sent to 148 Squadron even after such a great loss of airmen:

To 334 Wing (R) B.A.F.   434/18
From: HQ M.A.A.P. S.S.O.
JO8388 August 17, 1944 Top Secret:

"Should like you personally and all concerned in 334 Wing 148 Squadron and 1586 Flight to know how much I appreciate and admire their gallant efforts to help the underground army in Warsaw. Even in peace conditions it would be a tremendous flight with the addition of night fighters and flak it is one that could only be undertaken by crews with expert training and high courage. Deeply regret your heavy losses but hope some crews are safe and I know you realize your sacrifices are not in "vein" well done all British and Polish".

CYPHER TELEGRAM 172010B Signal received giving information of the crew of JP162. The date of the loss is written as 4-5 June It should be 4-5 August.

To: 30 Mission
From Air Ministry.   AX 381   17 Dec. 1944
Halifax JP 162 crashed near WARSAW 4-5 June

Crew as follows:-

117340	A/F/Lt. McCall, J.G.	X
C11369	F/O Anderson, P.J	
R131742	Sgt. Peterson, R.O.	√
1432309	Sgt. Jolly, A	√
1623931	Sgt. Underwood, W.C.	√
2219115	Sgt. Rae, J.F.	
2206350	Sgt. Aspinall, C	

H.Q. WARSAW state that McCall and two sergeants burned to death. Three senior NCOs were rescued and hidden. Fate of Anderson is unknown. No further news received to date. Signal any information Obtainable.

CYPHER TELEGRAM – IM 171502Z
To: 30 Mission
From: Troopers
SECRET
57998   MI9   8 Jan 1945   1400

Following Army and RAF personnel reported to be safe with
Polish Home Forces. We suggest you pass to Soviet military
authorities for purpose of identification if subsequently handed
over to Soviet partisan or regular army units:-

Army: No 1 to 15 entered on the list are army personnel.

RAF   Serial No.

16.	162391	Sgt. UNDERWOOD, W.C. RAF
19.	10386626	F/Sgt. DAVIS, Walter G. RAF
20.	1187031	F/Sgt. ELKINGTON-SMITH, E RAF
21.	1432309	Sgt. JOLLY A. RAF

RCAF Serial No.

| 23. | 131742 | F/Lt. PETERSON, R.O. Attd RCAF |

There are 5 RCAF not listed on my copy plus 1 RAAF

55-G/5

Embassy
Admiral
Air

I have only included the names of the airman, who have
connections to Halifax JP162,

APPENDIX C

The following are letters written after the war between a Polish partisan to two airmen he knew and helped.

Transcription of Letter from Polish from Mr. Jacek Popiel to Sgt. Charlie Underwood:

Mr. Popiel was at the age of 16 a member of the partisan group that helped the airmen of JP162.

Zabrze,30th 1990.

"Dear Charlie,

Thank you very much for your letter with very interesting materials. Excuse me that I answer so late. In Spring and summer I am busy with aero club/I fly by gliders as pilot and non professional instructor/and in my garden.

Now I write to you because on the 20th October I will fly to London. I will stay at my friend's house. I stay at home in the evenings. During the days I seek materials in London Archives.

I think that you made one mistake I remember and in our documents is written that in our battalion-1st bat.16th inf. reg. A.K., commandant capt."Lewila" there were 4 airmen. Two English and two Canadians, from the same crew. After Jammna battle, when the battalion was dissected two airmen went to

Plesna/Alan Jolly and Peterson/and two to another village/ Janowice? /.

When Red Cross came to our region my brother saw 4 UK fliers in Tarnow. Your pass from Cracow police to the rallying point in Rzeszow- Jasiona/Airbase/was compendet for four persons.

What do you say about this matter?

Now I write a letter to Mr. A Jolly. It would be good to make a small meeting in London. In London lives too Lt. "Mimosa", commandant 1-st company our battalion/ the last living commandant of the companies.

Do you have the escape button compass or escape plastic box? My Polish friend which flew many times to Warsaw gave me an escape cartes of Europe and carte for air aid pigeon post.

See you in London. My compliments to Mrs. Underwood."

Jacek Popiel

Copy of letter send from Charlie Underwood sent to Mr Popiel:

"Dear Jacek,

Thank you for your letter which I received with much interest. It is so nice to hear from friends after so many years especially one such as you who apart from risking so much fighting for the freedom of your country, took so many more risks caring for men as myself who were shot down over Poland whilst dropping supplies to the "AK". I have vivid memories of my months I spent in the Tarnow area of Poland, being care for by the patriots such as yourself, of the times spent in the forests and the marches. You say you have a photo of two Englishmen with Wachmistrz Lawina and a Jew who was hiding in his home.

I lived in a house in Tarnow in December 1944 to January 1945 with Mr. Anderson who was my navigator I cannot remember the last name but they had two sons Jesyk and Rudi and they were also hiding a Jewish girl. Could it be the same house I was in?

I have become a member of the Warsaw 44 club. The club has been trying to get a Memorial erected in Warsaw the area in which many English and polish aircraft were shot down and it is hoped that members of the Club will be going over for the dedication I will most surely be on that trip.

I am sorry I do not know the address of Mr, Anderson or Mr. Peterson who both went back to Canada after the war. I can give you the address of Mr. A. Jolly.

I am enclosing some photographs and other papers which I hope will be of interest to you together with an account so far as I can remember of our last flight. One paper is a cutting from the Dzennik Poski dated November 19, 1946 which is a photo of the grave of the three of our crew who lost their lives that night.

Thank you for writing to me and I hope we will be able to meet one another again some day in the future."

Yours Sincerely,

Charles Underwood

I did not receive your letter until the end of January

Undated translated from Polish letter to Alan Jolly.

"Dear Alan

I got your address from Charlie Underwood—Nottingham I was a soldier of 1st partisan battalion of 16th inf. reg. Polish Home Army—A.K. commandant Capt. "Lewila.

I served platoon protect of battalion commandant. In Jamna village where we stayed in Sept. 1944 four airmen-two English and two Canadians came to us. They had revolvers a Albion and Smith and Wesson and a plastic escape box in pocket on battledress. We all slept in the school garret and ate from one kettle. It was you and friends from the same crew.

When on the end of September1944 the battalion was dissected two fliers were going to Plesna and two to Janowice village?

I was the youngest soldier of battalion 16 years old I met you every day.

Charlie asserts that in our battalion were only he and F/O Anderson I remember and in our documents is written that there were four airmen from the same crew.

When Red Army came to our region my brother saw four UK fliers in Tarnow.

What do you say about this matter?

I have a photo with you Robert Peterson Lawina and a Jew in this home in Plesna This Jew being KGB agent killed in home after war.

On the 20th October I will fly to London. I will stay at my friend's house. I stay at home in the evenings. During the days

I seek materials in London Archives/ to the book. They carried aid for fighting. You can answer me at this address by letter or telephone

Do you still have escape button or plastic escape box? My Polish friend which flew many times to Warsaw gave me an escape button".

Jacek Popiel

APPENDIX D

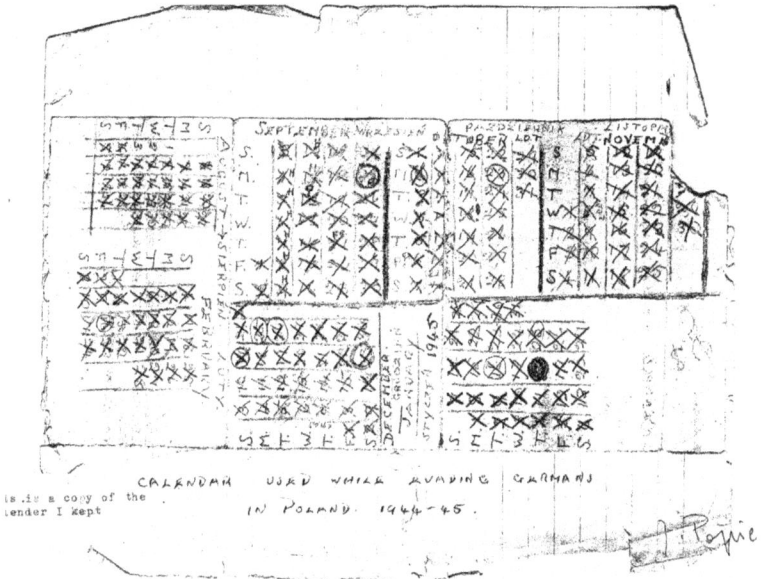

Calendar kept by Sgt C Underwood during his days of evading the Germans August 5th 1944 March 1945. Courtesy of Jacek Popiel.

Appendix E

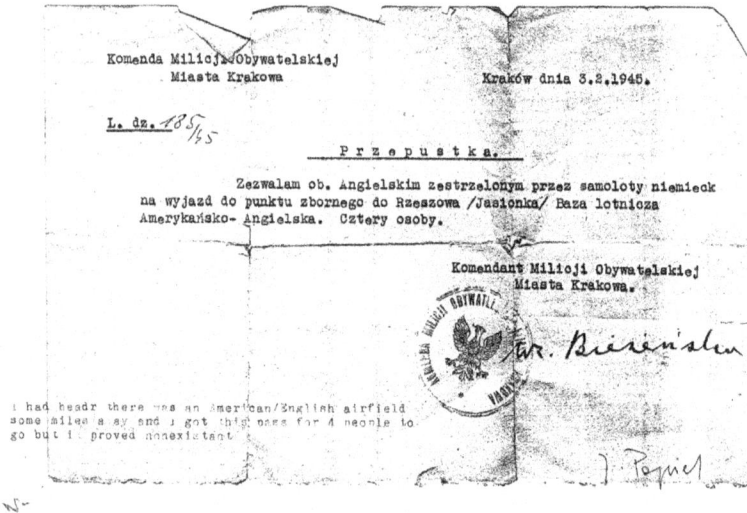

Travel Document issued for transport which proved a ruse as no
airfield existed. Courtesy of Jacek Popiel.

"The Warsaw run was the stuff which nightmares are made from"
The long flight over enemy territory and then an intense reception near
Warsaw, then the return flight.

The Poland Run.

NOTES

Chapter 1

I obtained the following information from records within **Scotlandspeople.org** website which can be downloaded and printed on home computer.

1. 1881 National Census records.

2. Michael and Catherine Marriage Banns, information.

Families in British India Society (FIBIS)

3. Obtained from FIBIS the passenger list information for the SS Lissmoyne which would take Michael and Catherine Rae to Madras, India.

4. The Baptismal certificates for the children born in India FIBIS Baptism indexes Madras Indexes 1860-1871.

5. "Taking the Queens Shilling" This was a monitory incentive offered to a serving soldier to reenlist for a further tour of duty. Queen Victoria was on the throne at that time thus the "Queens Shilling."

6. Find My Past website by using this site I was able to obtain copies of Michael Rays Army service records.

Chapter 2

7. Information taken from Family Tree started by Margaret Clow sister of John Rae and added and amended by author can be found on Genes Reunited website.

8. John Rae Merchant Seaman Record from Find My Past website.

9. Alice Johnson information was from spoken recollections of family and Family Records.

10. Thomas Johnson a deputy at Ellington information obtained from a visit to the Miners Museum, Ashington, Northumberland.

Chapter 3

11. "Fall Weiss or Plan White" a plan devised by Hitler which the German troops would carry out on September 1st 1939 to invade Poland. Information about this plan and the beginning of WW2 hostilities was sourced from History. com and Wikipedia.

12. Wehrmacht this was the German National Armed Force. Hitler who assumed the role as the Reich President and held supreme command of the armed forces, In 1935 Germany openly flouted military restructure and broke the Versailles treaty about the reaming of Germany. German re armament began 16 March and conscription into the armed forces on 21 May 1935.

13. War Effort was started to encourage the British population to help in anyway they could by volunteering as Air Raid Wardens, accommodating service men and women in their homes, collecting scrap metal etc.

14. Billet this was board and lodging for troops in a non military building.

15. Ration cards at the outbreak of WW2 the populations had to register with a chosen shop and were then given a book of coupon's. Each store was given enough food etc for each of the customers who had registered with them. Items were bought and coupons were cancelled in this way it ensured everyone would be able to purchase the basics.

16. John Rae reports for service information from Form 543 RAF Service Records.

17. Anson Aircraft were small training aircraft which airmen training to be air gunners flew in to practice their gunnery skills.

18. Martinet Aircraft these were Miles 25 aircraft specially built for RAF for the roll of towing targets.

Chapter 4

Special Note:

David Birrall, Director of Library/Archives/Displays from the Bomber Command Museum of Canada, Nanton, Alberta, Canada was a helpful source of information when I wrote to him and asked for help about Air Gunners Training. He kindly gave me permission to use information held by the museum in this chapter.

Chapter 5

19. Pilot James McCall's commission Form 543 McCall's Service records.

20. John Rae's letters to sister private collection of letters owned by author.

21. Mediterranean/ Middle East postings taken from a RAF Report by MA Barrow requested by the author.

Chapter 7

Special Note:

Larry Toft was a helpful source for information about the crew stations on the Halifax. He kindly supplied the pictures of the crew stations. As a Veteran pilot of 148 Special Duties Squadron he has a great knowledge of the mighty Halifax aircraft. Through correspondence between and Larry Toft and his two gunners I was able to get a clear picture of the workings of the plane being flown by the McCall crew.

Chapter 8

22. All information about the seven members of the crew of JP162 was obtained from RAF Form 453 which was the service records of the airmen. Further information was obtained from Evasion Reports at the National Archives in London, Commonwealth War Graves Commission and from surviving family members I was able to contact.

Chapter 9

23. RAF 148 Squadron information in this chapter was obtained from RAF Historian website records.

The following aircraft were flown by 148 Squadron during its history as a squadron. These brief notes can be expanded by further reading on Wikipedia website.

24. Audax: this was a Hawker developed as a trainer/reconnaissance aircraft It did not see combat action.

25. Wellesley: aircraft: another aircraft produced by Vickers It was a light bomber originally from a design for a general purpose aircraft It was flown mainly in the Middle East.

26. Wellington: this was made by Vickers Armstrong at Brooklands, Weybridge and was a twin engine, long range modern bomber. It was built in record time as part of the British propaganda but was displaced by the "Heavies" Lancaster and Halifax aircraft.

27 Liberator: Known as the B24 a USA heavy bomber designed and built by Consolidated Aircraft in San Diego, California and was used to fly long haul cargo flights between Canada and Prestwick, Scotland.

28. Lysander: used on special missions for dropping agents at small unprepared airstrips.

Chapter 11

29. Air bases were set up in Southern Italy which allowed RAF Special Duties Squadrons to make the supply drops.

30. Aircrew life and living conditions at Brindisi sourced from Torretta Flier magazine.

31. Missions Chart for the McCall crew was obtained from RAF Historian Records.

32. All information of flights made by McCall crew obtained from Squadron Record Books for the months of June through August 1944 AIR 27/996.

Chapter 12

33. Warsaw Uprising Documents sourced for signals from Churchill to Stalin during the Warsaw Uprising.

34. Uprising Accounts of Pryor and Slessor were sourced form 148 Squadron records and Flights of the Forgotten by K. Merrick page 208/209.

Chapter 13

35. Bienkiecki Kajetan Lotnicze Wsparcie Armii Krajowe Map showing the crash sites of August 4/5th 1944 mission.

36. Information about mission, crash and evasion crew of JP162 was researched from 148 Squadron Record Books AIR 27/996 Evasion Reports WO 208/3298-3327 WO 208/5405/5436.

37. MI9 report given by Sgt Walter Davis on return to England.

38. My Granddads Story personal recollection by Walter Davis and Sharon Spencer, Personal recollection by Flt. Sgt Robert Peterson.

Chapter 14

39. Letters received from Government offices relating to John Rae status as MIA and later KIA and details of burial in Poland.

All other information in this chapter was obtained from Rae family history and personal recollection of author.

Chapter 19

40. Information was about the losses of RAF aircrew and aircraft on August 4/5th 1944 mission was confirmed by checking the Harrington Aviation Museum Society and from 148Squadron record books AIR 27/996.

BIBLIOGRAPHY

General reading:

Bor-Komorowski   The Secret Army. Battery Press 1984.

Bienkiecki, Kajetan   Lotnicze Wsparcie Armii Krajowe.

Brooks Hubert   The Life and Times.

Derus, Stanislaw   Szli Partyzanci 2012.

Davis, Norman   Rising '44 the battle for Warsaw. Pan
                        Books 2004.

Cosby, Rita   Quiet Hero. Simon and Schuster 2010.

Congdon, Phillip   Behind the Hanger Doors. Sonik Books
                        1985.

Halley James A.   Royal Air Force Aircraft JA100-JZ999.
                        Air-Britain Publication 1990.

Merrick K.A.   Flights of the Forgotten Arms &
                        Armour Press 1989

Tadeusz Pelczynski   Armia Krajowa (AK Army Booklet)
                        March 2007.

RAF Squadron Website

RAF Hendon Museum Balkan Air Force information.

148 Squadron Website Squadron History.

C.W.G.C.   Commonwealth   War   Graves
                         Commission.

War Graves of the British Commonwealth 1939-1945 Book
Updated 1981.

C.W.W.G   Cemeteries in Poland and Union of the
                         Soviet Socialist Republic.

Air Gunner Training   Bomber Command Museum of
                         Canada, Nanton, Alberta, Canada,
                         David Burrell Director of Lib./
                         Archives/Displays.

Further Information Obtained from:

Rae Family Letters and Photographs
Scotland's People Website
FIBIS (Families in British India Society) website.
Air Crew Remembrance Society   Kelvin Youngs.

War and Game Website was a source for information for
No 148 Special Duties Squadron attached to the Balkan
Air Force.

National Archives, London for obtaining the following:
RAF 148 Squadron ORB's Operation Record Books May to
August 1944, Air 27/996
RAF 148 Squadron Record Books 1943 through August 1944
Air 27/996.

Evasion Reports (WO 208/3298-3327 & WO208/5405-5436)
I obtained
MI9 Reports for Sgt Charles Underwood RAFVR, Flt. Sgt.
Robert Orlando Peterson RCAF, F/O. Phillip James Anderson
RCAF, Sgt Walter Davis RAFVR.

RAF Service Record Form 543 of Sgt John Frederick Cairney
Rae RAFVR.
RAF Service Record Form 543 of Flt. Lt. James Girvan McCall,
RAFVR.
RAF Service Record Form 543 of Sgt Clifford Aspinall,
RAFVR.

Harrington Aviation Museum Society Allied Aircraft Lost on
Special Duties Operations. www.harringtonmuseum.org.uk.
"My Granddads Story" Personal Recollection by Walter Davis
and Sharon Spencer.
Personal Recollection by Josef Koszyk, Niecew, Poland.
Josef Koszyk provided Information/Photo of original Grave
site in Wojnarowa, Poland.
Personal Recollection by Jan Mika, Wojnarowa, Poland.
Paul Frasier grandson of Flt. Lt. James Girvan McCall RAFVR.
Robert Jolly son of Sgt. Alan Jolly RAFVR.
Robert Reichert of Krakow Poland.
Agnieszka Partridge, Journalist.
Thomak Jastrzębski and Jacek Popiel provided Evasion
documents of Sgt Charles Underwood RAFVR.
Revelstoke Museum, Revelstoke B.C Canada provided a News
article about Flt.Sgt. Robert O Peterson, RCAF.
Macloud Newspaper website Fort Maccloud Alberta Canada
recently provided information about Flt Sgt Peterson, RCAF
being presented Bomber Command Clasp Sept 2013.
Wikipedia Searches.
Warsaw Uprising Documents. This was the source for signals
from Churchill to Stalin during Warsaw Uprising.
Royal Canadian Air Force Website.

Information obtained from Operations Dark of the Moon Website and the following members:

Steve Alves provided photograph of the Camp at Brindisi taken by his father Roger Alves who served as ground crew with 148 Squadron in Brindisi.
John Heaton kindly gave permission for use of photographs from the Heaton Collection.
Steve Ellis gave permission for the use of photos from the Ellis Collection.
Larry Toft a Veteran of 148 Squadron provided photos of the Halifax Crew Stations.
Jennifer Elkin provided evasion report/ information about Sgt. Walter Davis one of the aircrew of Halifax JP 224.
France Gates recently provided some interesting information about a website created with information gathered by Hubert Brooks RCAF.
Toretta Flyer Magazine No 23 Winter edition was the source information about Brindisi.
Missing Believed Killed by Terry Marker founder of "Operation Dark of the Moon" a website which he founded which provides information about RAF 148 Special Duties Squadron. He also provided the source for photos of the Halifax production at Park Royal.

ACKNOWLEDGEMENTS

There are so many people who I need to thank and hopefully I will do so without forgetting anyone. Many people on hearing about my research and the information I had found about my dad John Rae encouraged me to put all this together in the form of a book.

Iain Macpherson has been a friend for over 30 years. He is an avid aircraft enthusiast who worked in the aerospace industry until his retirement. He has helped in researching the history of 148 Squadron and the Halifax flown by my dad especially the rear gun turret. His constant encouragement and his suggestion to keep a diary during my visit to Krakow led to his question when I returned "Now what are you going to do with all this information?" helped me begin this long journey. Thanks Iain.

Operations Dark of the Moon website did not exist when I first began tracing my fathers Royal Air Force Service during WW2 and it was only after I had decided to reopen my files and dig a little deeper that I came across the site Terry Marker had founded. The members are all connected in some way to 148 Special Duties Squadron. To each and every one of you who have helped in anyway many thanks for all the great information. Special thanks to Terry Marker who has kindly spent time sending me information about the building of Halifax JP 162. His wonderful quotes and encouragement have spurred me on. Steve Andrews has given great support and helped post the few pictures I had of my dad on the website. Larry Toft, a veteran from 148 Squadron, and his gunners Dave Lambert and Jim McKenzie Leith were one of the crews who flew to Brindisi to replace the crews lost on the August 4/5, 1944 Mission. Larry has a wealth of first hand information and has provided me with information with the help of his crew about the "crew stations" in the Halifax as well as photographs. I am pleased to call him a friend. Piotr Hoyda from Poland who is also a member provided me with information about my dad's service when I was struggling to find any. Thanks Piotr you set me on the right track. France Gates provided information to help in my searches in tracing crew members and their families. Jennifer Elkin has been a great source of encouragement and also information especially in coming to my rescue with the technical details of preparing the images for this book. Our friendship has been cemented by connections we have had in our past when I suddenly thought "I know that name!" Thanks for all your help and your friendship.

Kris and Angnieszka Partridge found me to ask questions about one of the airmen of Halifax JP162. They are both busy people. Kris works for the BBC and Agnieszka working in Krakow as a journalist and writer. They shared information which added credence to my story. Agnieszka has recently written and published a book about Plesna which has a chapter about JP162 and the evading aircrew who had been housed nearby. She was able to share a photograph of two of the crew who evaded capture. Being able to meet with her in Krakow was a pleasure and an added bonus. To Kris who I was able to meet on my last visit to England thank you for the wonderful day spent visiting Runnymede and Windsor.

A owe a big thank you to Karl Kjarsgaard of Bomber Command Museum in Canada. In my searches for information about the Canadian airmen of my aircrew, Karl wrote to me offering information of sites to search. His knowledge about finding documents at the National Archives in London led me to finding the evasion reports of the crew who survived. When I contacted David Birrell also of the Bomber Command Museum in Nanton, Alberta who is the Director of Library/Archives/ Displays about Air Gunner training he was a helpful source of information and has allowed me to use this information in my book. I am hopeful that I will be able to visit the museum in the near future. Thank you both.

The National Archives Kew Staff provided a complete novice (myself) help in finding and copying the documents I was seeking on my visits to Kew. Thankfully I am now able to view and download some files from their website on my computer at home in California which is an added bonus.

Thank you to The Blackpool and Fylde Gazette Newspaper. Special Thanks to Craig Fleming who had a column called Memory Lane. After many unsuccessful attempts to trace families of the surviving airmen I contacted this newspaper and was pleasantly surprised that you printed my letter and equally surprised to get a response. Craig you went the extra mile to help. I wish you well in your retirement.

Robert Reichert what can I say about this young man. I found him by chance after seeing the beautiful and moving photographs he had taken on All Saints Day (November 1st) of the graves in the Commonwealth Section of Krakow Rakowicki Cemetery, where my father is buried, aglow with lanterns. Without asking he became my researcher in Poland of all things to be found about JP162 and most importantly my interpreter. His most recent accomplishment was to design the cover for this book. I believe that he has managed to capture and produce something very special. Robert without your help and encouragement I would not be writing this story. In the journey I have taken during these past two years you have also become a true friend.

To all the people we met during our visit to Poland in August 2013 your kindness and hospitality to a complete stranger will never be forgotten. To all the "unknown" people of Krakow who each year place a lantern on the graves of "the fallen" in the Allied section of Rakowicki Cemetery in Krakow a heartfelt thank you for remembering these brave men.

A very special thank you to Josef and Helena Koyzsk and their family the owners of the home built on the crash site in Niecew, Poland. Your kindness and hospitality, even though there were some language difficulties, will not be forgotten. You were able to find and share some missing pieces of information.

To Mr. Ostraga whom we met at the Koyzsk home thank you very much for the book you gave me about the AK Army.

I owe a debt of gratitude to Robert Springwald and the group of Aircraft Historians in Krakow for their efforts to get recognition from the Polish Government for the crew of my dad's plane Halifax JP 162FS.

Tomasz Jastrzebski and his wife Magda and their wonderful family welcomed me into their home and organized a wonderful week of visits. The documents he gave me and his searches to find out about the crew of this plane filled in many of the blanks.

Thank you to Zbignien Hajduk for coming to Krakow Airport with Mateusz and Beata Jastrzebski to meet us when we arrived after our long journey and for driving us to the Jastrzebski home the following day. Thank you to Marcin Bednarek whom we met during out visit to the Krakow Air Museum.

The curator and the staff of the Home Army Museum in Krakow provided a special tour which helped me to understand the struggles of the partisans. The surviving aircrew was helped by these groups so it gave me a good perspective on what their life must have been like and enabled me to write a more complete story. My visit to the Aircraft Museum in Krakow was equally interesting and again we were made welcome by the museum staff and given a tour by Kamil Stasiak a university student who is writing his dissertation on WW2 Aircraft.

Many thanks to Adam Sikorski and his camera crew from Polish National Television. Through the connection that Tomasz Jasrzebeski had with Adam Sikorski the TV crew returned to film my visit to Koszyk family home in Niecew (the crash site) and original grave site in Wojnarowa as a follow up to a TV documentary made in 2010.

Thank you Mr. Jan Mika who told his story of seeing the airplane crash and to his family who made us so welcome and provided cold drinks on a very hot day.

Shelagh Limmer agreed to become my proof reader and editor. Our connection is very special and she was able to share the visit to Krakow with me. Thank you for your help and suggestions. My daughters Michelle Bedard and Helen Kilday were able to give technical advice and support knowing full well my struggles with present day technology and gave suggestions with the layout and presentation of this book.

I have very happy memories of a special Aunt and Uncle Margaret and Charlie Clow. Without the precious letters and photographs Aunt Margaret gave me there would be no story. Lastly I remember my mother Alice Rae, as brave and strong woman who raised me with unconditional love.

To my family, Robert, my husband, who came to my rescue when I was trying to put my picture file together and assemble all the book documents to be published and my two daughters Michelle and Helen. Thank you for allowing me to make this Special Journey.

www.ingramcontent.com/pod-product-compliance
Lightning Source LLC
Chambersburg PA
CBHW022123080426
42734CB00006B/234